2

D0225868

Teaching Science to Children

Second Edition

SOURCE BOOKS ON EDUCATION
(VOL. 35)

GARLAND REFERENCE LIBRARY
OF SOCIAL SCIENCE
(VOL. 747)

Teaching Science to Children

Second Edition

Mary D. Iatridis

with a chapter by
Miriam Marecek

GARLAND PUBLISHING, INC. • NEW YORK & LONDON
1993

Library of Congress Cataloging-in-Publication Data

Iatridis, Mary D., 1928–
    Teaching science to children. — 2nd ed. / Mary D. Iatridis ; with
a chapter by Miriam Marecek.
       p. cm. — (Garland reference library of social science ;
vol. 747. Source books on education ; vol. 35)
    Includes index.
    ISBN 0-8153-0090-5
    1. Science—Study and teaching (Primary)—Bibliography.
2. Science—Juvenile literature—Bibliography. 3. Handicapped
children—Education—Science—Bibliography. I. Marecek, Miriam.
II. Title. III. Series: Garland reference library of social science;
v. 747. IV. Series: Garland reference library of social science.
Source books on education ; vol. 35.
Z5818.S3I24 1993
[LB1532]
016.3723'5044—dc20   92-28047
                                                          CIP

Printed on acid-free, 250-year-life paper
Manufactured in the United States of America

Contents

Preface

This book is a labor of love for children and science and it is based on the assumption that science learning for children is as essential as reading, writing, and arithmetic. The books reviewed reflect a commitment to this premise and, although authors may disagree on approaches, strategies, and content, they all make strong and convincing arguments for the contributions of science teaching to the intellectual development of children.

The golden era of science curriculum from the 1960s echoes throughout the bibliography, with the prevailing view that science be taught as a combination of process and content.

The book is written for educators of young children (teachers in traditional and non-traditional settings), with the idea that, through the multiplicity of approaches to teaching science presented in the book, they may search and identify the one most suitable to them.

It has been a challenge to track down books on how to teach science (Chapter II) and books with science activities that will engage children in learning science (Chapter III). At times it was hard to decide in which category to place certain books because of the intermingling of methodology and activities in their content. I hope my decision will not discourage the reader from using the books.

Finally, Chapter IV lists and reviews science books from children's literature, a contribution of Miriam Marecek, an educator and expert on children's literature of long standing. It is a selective bibliography of different types of books and topics. It will be of special interest to teachers and parents and will motivate children to read and find out about science-based topics.

Teaching Science to Children

I

How Science Contributes to Young Children's Thinking

When children actively explore their physical world, they have the potential to engage in thinking activities that are based on such scientific principles as observing, comparing, inventing, predicting, and experimenting. This brief chapter summarizes the constructivist view of how thinking emerges during childhood, especially how young children learn to think through their science-based explorations.[1]

Thinking occurs throughout life. It is influenced by experience and is interrelated with the life stages through which all people pass. As people mature, they engage in thinking about the past (remembering), understanding the present, and contemplating the future.[2]

It all begins shortly after birth, when infants bring meaning to their lives by exploring the world around them. From their explorations, they experience excitement and satisfaction and gain information that leads to knowledge—a process that, it is hoped, will last their lifetime.[3] According to Piaget, human beings develop cognitive structures through a four-stage sequence that varies qualitatively.[4]

Stage 1. At birth, infants are equipped with hereditary structures that are transformed into cognitive structures through the infants' complex interactions with their environments. For example, "hitting" a mobile suspended over a crib creates a reaction that causes an infant to try it over and over again. These repetitive activities establish a cognitive structure that is based on the connections between hitting the

3

mobile and the mobile's subsequent movements. Similarly, a hands-on experience with a ball (by viewing, touching, and mouthing it) contributes to the older infant's understanding of how a ball behaves; with further experiences—rolling, bouncing, and throwing a ball—the child extends his or her knowledge about it. In general, the child's innate curiosity is the self-initiated force through which the child is driven to engage in further hands-on experiences and explorations that lead to a greater understanding of the world.

Stage 2. Children's cognitive structures change with the development of representational forms of cognition and of language (two to three-year-olds). For example, children will recognize a ball in a picture and will then call out "ball" to evoke a response to get one. During this stage, thinking is bound by the sensory system and by egocentricity. The children's experiences in the physical world make sense to them when the children interact with objects in that world, and their cognitive structures expand and enrich them the more the children engage in hands-on explorations. For instance, the more kinds of balls children roll, bounce, kick, and throw, the broader understanding they have of how balls behave. At the sight of balls, children reflect (remember) which one is more "desirable" (bounces the most) and choose a ball on the basis of their understanding of how all kinds of balls operate.

Stage 3. During their years of "concrete operations" (six to seven-year-olds), children's thinking about the world becomes stable. During this stage, children develop concepts of the permanency of objects, the causes and effects of phenomena, and quantified relationships among objects and phenomena. For example, children can roll balls of different sizes and matter down a ramp and construct knowledge of which balls go fast, faster, slow, or slower. They can also examine them and decide why (cause) the various balls go down the ramp at different speeds. These experiences become the basis for determining the criteria for predicting how new balls will behave while going down a ramp, as the children compare the new balls with the ones they already know. Furthermore, in rolling the new balls down the ramp, children can find out whether their criteria (predictions) are valid or need to be modified. These intricate thinking processes are important for children's understanding of how the world operates. They also lead to the next stage of cognition, which is the basis for abstract thinking that lasts a lifetime.

Stage 4. This stage begins in preadolescence. In the context of balls and ramps, during this stage, children investigate balls beyond the ball's concrete attributes of weight, size, texture, and the like. They can abstract properties, such as friction, elasticity, and density, and make predictions based on assumptions about balls and ramps that go conceptually beyond what is visible. Observing, comparing, predicting, and experimenting are part of these intricate thinking processes that make science an exciting body of knowledge to discover.

For young children, thinking is closely bound to their physical actions because that is the way children learn about the world around them. The constructivist view not only supports such an approach, but recommends strategies for developing environments and increasing teachers' awareness to facilitate children's efforts to engage in physical-knowledge activities that contribute to such development.[5]

These assumptions validate young children's early science experiences, in which their initiatives in exploring, their actions with objects, and their observations and thoughts about objects are encouraged and valued. Just as in the physical-knowledge approach of the constructivist view, science for young children relies on the children's interactions with concrete objects and experiences with phenomena, so children can learn in the context of their development.

Children learn when their concrete experiences are connected to their world; when they explore objects or phenomena and observe what happens to them and how it happens; when they use their newly acquired knowledge from their exploration of one object (or phenomenon) to engage in a new situation to solve a new problem; when they communicate their findings—by talking about or drawing them, for example—and when they create new challenges, predict, and experiment. To engage children in such scientific investigations and thinking activities, adults must create an environment that is conducive to initiating them; that is, they must provide the appropriate materials and understand their roles in helping to make these activities happen.

Objects (both living and non-living) and phenomena that have the greatest potential to generate science-based behavior in children should be of interest to children, should stimulate their curiosity so they will be inspired to question, and should engage them in active investigations. These objects and phenomena must be open-ended to sustain multiple explorations. For example, with animals, children can investigate what they look like, what they eat, how they sleep, how they protect themselves, and how they move. With water, children can explore how to pour and squirt it and how it moves and changes direction and shape.

Another factor that influences children's thinking as they engage in scientific explorations is the role of adults as mentors who guide children through this process. To fulfill these roles, adults need to know how children learn at different developmental stages, how to organize and manage the environment in which children are involved, and which materials will enhance the children's involvement.

Adults can make use of several strategies to help children initiate and conduct their explorations. As observers, they may begin to understand the children's science-based involvement and listen to what the children say about their findings and their plans of what to do next. As supporters, they may encourage and facilitate children's interactions and thinking about their experiments-investigations and help children reach their own conclusions. As extenders, they may probe further, with such questions as: What will happen if . . . ? How did you do that? Can you do this with someone else? As extenders, adults can also engage children in reflecting on what they are doing or have done and encourage them to communicate their thinking about what they have found, how they found it, and what meaning it has for them. In sum, at all times, adults should validate and encourage children's investigative actions and thoughts.[6]

In conclusion, science can contribute to young children's critical thinking when they engage in hands-on, developmentally appropriate, physical explorations. Adults can enhance this development with appropriate responses, such as observing, supporting, and asking questions to extend children's explorations and challenging them to think about these explorations.

NOTES

1. Costa, Arthur L. *Developing Minds.* Alexandria, Va.: A.S.C.D., 1985.

2. Smith, Frank. *To Think.* New York: Teachers College Press, 1990.

3. *Ibid.*

4. Piaget, J. *The Origins of Intelligence.* New York: International Press, 1936/1952.

5. DeVries, Rheta, and Lawrence Kohlberg. *Constructivist Early Education.* (Chapter 4). Washington, D.C.: N.A.E.Y.C., 1990.

6. Iatridis, Mary, Jeff Winokur, and Karen Worth. Research in progress. *Teaching Science in Early Childhood Classrooms.* National Science Foundation, 1990–1993.

II

Textbooks

Introduction

Science teaching for children has been greatly influenced during the past 25 years by both the educational world and by scientific knowledge. More specifically, contributions to the field have been made from such areas as child development and learning theories, curriculum organization and development, materials and content, social attitudes and values, and evaluation systems. Textbooks on the subject reflect a wide variety of approaches, ranging from the teacher-centered view that the accumulation of factual scientific knowledge is the desirable outcome of children's learning to the child-centered discovery approach, in which the process and the children's experience themselves are the focus.

Child Development and Learning Theories

Essential to all books published on teaching science to children is the author's viewpoint on how children develop intellectually and how they learn effectively. The theories that prevail in most writing reflect those developed by Piaget, Bruner, and Gagne. Certain authors base the teaching of science on one theory more than another, while others rely on an eclectic model that incorporates each theory selectively.

Piaget's developmental theory explains how children learn in a sequence of stages and how each stage utilizes and assimilates the preceding stage. The four major stages are sensory-motor (0–3 years), preoperational (3–6 years), concrete operations (6–11 years), and formal operations (11 years to adult). The child's many experiences during each stage contribute greatly to his development. Piaget claimed that children must experience the physical world so that they may gain knowledge of it.

Children experience objects and physical phenomena and understand them according to their current developmental level. For example, children in the pre-operational stage explain the phenomena around them perceptually—"how they look"— and not logically—"how they really are"—which will be the understanding in later stages. We know that children at the early stage lack the ability to coordinate variables and cannot view the idea of an object having several properties; the concept of conservation has not developed yet and the child cannot reverse thought.[1]

The author's view on child development has a serious impact on the organization of science curriculum and the teaching strategies that are used. From a Piagetian perspective, children's interactions with the physical world are important because children understand and learn about the properties of materials and phenomena through their experiences. For example, materials sink or float as the child works with them in a water environment; young children will predict that large things will sink, while older students may have different comments.

If Piaget focused on children's developmental stages, Jerome Bruner examined "the act of learning." His widely quoted hypothesis that "any subject can be taught effectively in some intellectually honest form to any child at any stage of development" has greatly influenced the structure and organization of science curricula in schools. The learning process according to Bruner is a three-stage sequence: (1) the individual's information acquisition, (2) the transformation or manipulation of this information by the individual in determining whether it serves adequately the new tasks,[2] and

(3) "the learning episode" is accommodated, depending on the capabilities of the learner. This theory accommodates children at different developmental stages and suggests a spiral sequence of curriculum so that the act of learning for the same content can be reenacted several times through the course of the child's life. For example, magnets can be taught several times because the "act of learning" for the child will be a new one each time.

Another theorist who examined the act of learning in a more systematic way is Robert Gagne. He considered the process of scientific research, adapted it to the teaching of science to children, and concluded that scientific inquiry is the most desirable learning process for students to follow when they study science.[3] Furthermore, he claimed that scientific inquiry as a process for learning science can be applied to younger students, provided the conditions of instruction employed comply with the goals appropriate for that age group.

Scientific inquiry proceeds in a stage-like manner. This systematic, problem-solving, thinking process can begin with children at the kindergarten level when they begin to acquire competencies that contribute to the process of scientific inquiry. The competencies the learner must acquire to proceed with the inquiry method include observing, figuring, measuring, orienting things in space, describing and classifying objects and events, inferring, and making conceptual models.[4] Such competencies are only the beginning of learning and do not confine their usefulness to science alone but to any body of knowledge where inquiry can be applied.

Criteria in Organization and Development

In the organization and development of science curriculum, there are two prevailing approaches: the inquiry process that Gagne promoted and the child-centered approach that builds on Piagetian developmental theory.

The science curriculum based on Gagne arranges subject matter or content in a hierarchical fashion. Gagne provides evidence that learning materials can be planned and sequenced in a way similar to the scientific process. This learning model has been the basis for a science curriculum like S-APA (Science-A Process Approach) developed by the National Science Foundation (NSF) in the mid-1960s.[5]

The child-centered emphasis focuses on children's developmental levels, takes into account children's views about the physical world, and builds on them. Although inquiry is incorporated in child-centered curricula, the emphasis remains on the way the children explore the materials and how they integrate them into their lives. The ESS (Elementary Science Study) is an example of a child-centered science curriculum that was also developed by the National Science Foundation in the mid-1960s.[6]

The books reviewed generally reflect one of these two approaches. Other works cited employ a combination of the two.

Content and Materials

It is widely accepted that interactions with materials are essential in the teaching of science so that children can learn about the properties of objects as well as other physical phenomena. During the 1960s, the NSF funded four major science curriculum programs for children in grades K–8: COPES (Conceptually Oriented Program in Elementary Science), ESS (Elementary Science Study), S-APA (Science—A Process Approach), and SCIS (Science Curriculum Improvement Study). These programs relate closely to prevailing theories of learning. The content and materials for all programs aim to enhance children's conceptual thinking and understanding of science by using the process of scientific inquiry.

The literature in early childhood education supports the idea that varied science experiences for young children are effective ways for learning science, especially when they relate to the environment with which the children are familiar. The quality of the experience depends on the materials and how they are presented. It is important for young children to engage in sensory explorations because their sensory systems are their investigating tools. Therefore, sensory observations and perceptual discrimination assist in the sorting of objects and phenomena that are desirable outcomes of the inquiry process.[7]

"What kind of science?" becomes more of an issue during the elementary grades. The viewpoints on what science to teach are diverse and are reflected in science sourcebooks and in the four programs created by the NSF.

Social Attitudes and Values

One of the reasons why the quality and content of science teaching varies from school to school can be directly attributed to the societal forces that influence curriculum in schools. The local management of the educational process is responsible for the type of science programs that prevail in a school. As a result, in recent times environmental concerns have increased the teaching of ecology, nutrition, and the effects of pollution and nuclear fallout. In her book *Teaching Science as a Continuous Inquiry*, Mary B. Rowe alerts educators to the fact that "science is the central enterprise of the societies populating the planet earth during the 20th century" and cautions educators to "find out how science is affecting us and what we can do about it."[8] It appears that, for some educators, the social implications are the focus of science teaching, while others look at scientific literacy and education as a key to national supremacy in the technological race.

Regardless of orientation, societal forces control budgetary sources and, as a result, have a direct effect on "what science" should be taught to children. It should be noted that not all the books on how to teach science indicate concerns about value implications in science curriculum.

Evaluation Systems

The implementation of a science curriculum is closely related to its method of evaluation. Evaluation techniques are widely discussed in most textbooks and are as diverse as the answers to "why science for children?" Guidelines for evaluation come from various sources. Some curriculum developers follow Bloom's taxonomy in setting objectives and devising instruments to measure the effectiveness of achieving these objectives. Other educators consider the overt behavior of the children as the source of evaluation. However, the problems of reliability and validity in such observational methodology hinder the promotion of science programs that favor the interactive process as the focal point of teaching science. No doubt, pressure for accountability favors science programs that provide measuring devices like tests, while other programs with more appeal to teachers and children have been curtailed because there has been a lack of credible evaluative data.

In summary, the books that have emerged as textbooks in the teaching of science to children during the past 25 years reflect a gamut of teaching methodologies. For example, a book such as E. Victor's classic *Science for the Elementary School* represents an eclectic model in the teaching of science. It informs teachers of the theories explaining children's learning and their implications for teaching strategies. The guidelines indicate how the "process of science" has become more than the "content." The emphasis on the "process of science" as a basis for curriculum organization and teaching strategy prevails in most books that qualify as textbooks on teaching science to children. The differences among these books can be found in the organization and implementation of the inquiry process and in the content recommended for teaching.

"Scientific and social inquiry go hand in hand in the world we now face," claims Mary B. Rowe.[9] She emphasizes the need for integrating science in our everyday teaching because of the effect science has on our everyday living. Furthermore, she recommends that children be taught the scientific process in relation to issues that affect daily life, such as pollution, nutrition, and ecology.

Child-centered considerations in teaching science prevail in Doris A. Trojcak's book *Science with Children*.[10] She states that affective and cognitive goals must intermingle. The attitudes of teachers toward science must also be dealt with and their fears resolved so that science will have an appeal to them and they in turn will facilitate children's science learning.

This is only a sample of the range of content and viewpoints that appear in the many existing books in science teaching.

NOTES

1. Chittenden, Ed A. "Piaget in Elementary Science Education." *Science and Children* 8, No.4 (Dec. 1970), 9–15.

2. Bruner, Jerome. *The Process of Education.* Cambridge, Mass.: Harvard UP, 1960.

3. Gagne, R. "The Learning Requirements for Enquiry." *Journal of Research in Science Teaching* 1, Issue 2 (1963), 144–153.

4. *Ibid.*

5. Waters, Barbara S. *Science Can Be Elementary.* New York: Citation, 1973.

6. *Ibid.*

7. Landsdowne, Brenda, et al. *Teaching Elementary Science.* New York: Harcourt Brace Jovanovich, 1971; Elkind, David. "Piaget and Science Education." *Science and Children* 10, No.3 (Nov. 1972), 9–12.

8. Rowe, Mary B. *Teaching Science as a Continuous Inquiry: A Basic.* 2nd ed. New York: McGraw-Hill, 1978.

9. *Ibid.*

10. Trojcak, Doris A. *Science with Children.* New York: McGraw-Hill, 1979.

BIBLIOGRAPHY

Abruscato, Joseph. *Teaching Children Science.* Englewood Cliffs, N.J.: Prentice Hall, 1982.

The book is organized in three parts. Part I analyzes theories of how children learn science, discusses teaching and curriculum models, expands on assessment techniques, and suggests ways to adapt the teaching of science for handicapped and gifted children. Parts II and III focus on science content activities and methods. Earth, space, atmosphere, weather, the cosmos, life sciences, and physical science are fully developed topics. The chapters on ecology and energy are particularly interesting. The appendixes include Piagetian tasks, the metric system, and references to suppliers of science materials and books on science teaching. The book has a lively style and offers practical suggestions for effective science teaching. The wide range of topics can be appropriate for grades K-6 and will interest teachers who want to venture seriously into science teaching.

Almy, Millie. *Logical Thinking in the Second Grade.* New York: Teachers College Press, 1970.

The contribution of Almy to science education is extensive. She researched "how children think," utilizing science materials and phenomena and Piagetian developmental theory. A most valuable book for the science educator who wants documentation through research.

Anastasiou, Clifford J. *Teachers, Children and Things: Materials-Centered Science.* Minneapolis, Minn.: Holt, Rinehart and Winston of Canada, 1971.

The book is concerned with the interaction between children and materials during the scientific process. It describes activities for children and offers tips to teachers on how to help them get involved. The author bases his teaching theories on children's developmental stages and draws from the psychological constructs of Piaget's developmental theory and Torraine's work on creativity. A teacher can facilitate inquiry and discovery through materials found inside and outside the classroom. A flow chart on school grounds from the Nuffield Teachers Guide on page 82 emphasizes further the openness of this book. Its informal style is most valuable for the teacher of young children who has been apprehensive about teaching science.

Anderson, Ronald. *Developing Children's Thinking Through Science*. Englewood Cliffs, N.J.: Prentice Hall, 1970.

This book takes a systematic approach to the relationship between science teaching and children's thinking. It examines a sequence of philosophical constructs on the question of what is science. The book questions the belief that behavioral objectives are the only approach to effective science teaching and expands on the characteristics of problem-solving and creativity in this field.

The author acknowledges the importance of developmental stages (Piaget) and the hierarchy of learning (Gagne) and urges teachers to consider them in planning science teaching. In curriculum design and resources, Anderson offers a wide range of theoretical and practical alternatives. He addresses teachers' "areas of vital concern" during the teaching of science and concludes with a wide range of evaluation guidelines. The book offers a very thorough examination of all the issues that relate to the teaching of science to children. It will be useful to concerned teachers who want to go beyond lesson plans and understand how children learn science and who further wish to be effective as teachers of science.

Beaty, Seddon Kelly, and Irene Fountas. *Butterflies Abound: A Whole Language Resource Guide*. Lexington, Mass.: Early Education Curriculum, 1990.

Organized in a teachable sequence, this paperbound book presents a thematic approach to learning about a central, science-based topic—butterflies. The material is developmentally appropriate for children in the primary grades.

The science of a butterfly is experienced by the children in the context of their lives. The skills demanded for problem solving, critical thinking, scientific investigations, art projects, and oral and written language are actively taught as the children learn about butterflies.

An exhaustive web of ideas for each subject area sets the stage for the teaching-learning experience. The science content is organized in a series of concepts and the strategies for learning reflect the integration of the curriculum. The children's work is the key to evaluation.

Special sections on math, language arts, social studies, music, dramatic play, art, physical activity, and cooking provide a variety of vehicles for learning more about butterflies. A glossary, bibliographies, and the appendixes are also useful resources.

Blough, G.O., and Julius Schwartz. *Elementary School Science and How to Teach It.* 7th ed. New York: Holt, Rinehart and Winston, 1984.

This book, addressed to teachers of elementary grades who teach science, is comprehensive and includes vast amounts of scientific information. The first part is relatively brief (100 pages) and offers an overview of what elementary science is and how it can be taught. Techniques, strategies, and resources are discussed and recommended. The remainder of the book (approximately 500 pages) offers science content classified into the areas of earth, universe, living things, matter, and energy. Each topic is discussed in terms of content and teaching strategies.

Butts, David P. *Teaching Science in the Elementary School.* New York: The Free Press, 1975.

This book is more concerned with involving children in learning science than with the traditional overviews of goals, strategies, techniques, and resources that usually appear in science teaching books. In Part I the author states his philosophy and objectives, creating the framework for guiding and assessing the children's learning. Part II contains powerful ideas on how to involve children in learning through activities derived from the well-known science curricula of SCIS, S-APA, and ESS. A science teacher will find this section most valuable. Butts expresses his viewpoints through many anecdotal situations and assists teachers in developing views, values, and judgments on teaching science to children.

Butts, David P., ed. *Research and Curriculum Development in Science Education.* Austin, Tex.: University of Texas Press, 1970.

An in-depth monograph on research in the teaching and learning of science. The research components focus on the educational experience and its consequences for learning. A significant contribution for scholars in science education who want to further their own research in the field of evaluation of science teaching.

Butts, David P., and Gene E. Hall. *Children and Science: The Process of Teaching and Learning.* Englewood Cliffs, N.J.: Prentice Hall, 1975.

Organized in an innovative, self-directed manner, the book aims to instruct through activities that enable the reader to experience and understand the skills necessary for effective science learning. Some of the activities are selected from the well-known NSF science education programs—ESS, SCIS, S-APA, Minnemast, and others—and demonstrate the diversity of approach and philosophy in the programs. The chapters are titled informally: "Science is . . . ," "Using Your Senses," "Telling Another Person," "Finding Out How Much More," "Communicating Change," "Explaining What You Observe," "Concluding an Experiment," "Causes and Effects," "Defining Terms," "Searching for Patterns," "Generalizing," and "Scientist at Work." The writing style has a sense of immediacy that is reinforced by the conversational tone of the author. The book is enjoyable and helpful, especially for the teacher who may feel overwhelmed at the idea of teaching science to children.

Cain, Sandra E., and Gail M. Evans. *Sciencing: An Involvement Approach to Elementary Science Methods.* 2nd ed. Columbus, Ohio: Merrill, 1984.

Process skills are a feature of this book. The authors introduce each chapter with a flowchart so that the reader is guided through its content. Chapter One summarizes the nature of science, children, and learning, and shows how an understanding of this material contributes to the planning and implementation of science teaching. Next follows a discussion of the place of the laboratory approach, textbooks, and text kits in science curricula. The NSF programs of the 1960s (S-APA, SCIS, and ESS) are reviewed as the classical laboratory approach curricula, and sample activities are presented from each of them. The strengths and weaknesses of all types of curricula are evaluated on the basis of well-stated criteria. Text kits are singled out as an acceptable alternative to science teaching. Teachers' lesson planning and classroom management are addressed and guidelines on teaching science for the handicapped are developed. The potential of microcomputers in science teaching receives special recognition.

Finally, the book offers a wide variety of appendixes. The most impressive is the review of the NSF Elementary Science Programs. They are presented historically, philosophically, and conceptually in a content sequence. The book includes everything you ever wanted to know about science and how to teach it to children. However, it requires a skilled reader of curricula body to utilize and appreciate its content. Its multiple charts and illustrations are exceptional.

Carin, Arthur A., and Robert B. Sund. *Teaching Science Through Discovery.* 4th ed. Columbus, Ohio: Merrill, 1980.

The authors suggest that the text be used as a reference book on teaching science through discovery and, indeed, the book fulfills such criteria. The first 15 chapters emphasize strategies and conditions for developing effective discovery lessons in science. Included are chapters on developing questioning and sensitive listening techniques and on creating and teaching discovery laboratory lessons. There is a survey of existing science programs that incorporate discovery strategies and plans for arranging classrooms to enhance individualized as well as group teaching. Children's developmental stages are considered and referred to throughout the book and special effort is made to address issues that relate to teaching science to preschoolers. Attention is given to integrating discovery science teaching with other subjects, and evaluating the discovery method. Each chapter concludes with examples that contribute to concept clarification. Illustrations and charts are helpful and attractive.

The remainder of the book covers the content areas of science—living, environmental, and physical. The format follows an investigative and discovery sequence that is most helpful to the teacher.

A special section is devoted to discovery activities for preschoolers. Piagetian tasks are presented as reference points for children's levels of understanding. One of the appendixes offers a valuable timeline of the history of science education in the United States.

Craig, Gerald S. *Science for the Elementary School Teacher.* 5th ed. Waltham, Mass.: Blaisdell, 1966.

The author addresses teachers on their responsibility to adapt the wonders of science to children's interests and capabilities. Some of the issues discussed are content learning vs. process in science teaching, how basic patterns of the

universe and nature relate to concept formation, the importance of interaction in science teaching, the place of science in a
democracy, and how the environment near the school can
contribute to science teaching. The major part of the book
focuses on the content of science: earth, the universe, life on
earth, energy of the universe. In the last 100 pages, the author
offers examples of good science teaching. He classifies concepts
and content by grade as they relate to the book. A teacher will
find useful the differences in teaching methods suggested for
each grade and the emphasis on children's development and
level of interest.

DeVito, Alfred. *Creative Wellsprings for Science Teaching, 2nd
Edition.* West LaFayette, Ind.: Creative Ventures, 1989.

"Creative" is one way to summarize this book. The author
combines "poetry" and pragmatism to explain what science is
and how it should be taught.

The book is organized in four sections. Section I briefly
introduces the topic What is science? The definition is dynamic
and goes beyond the process-content duality to show that "it's a
human enterprise."

Section II—Science Cornucopia/Extending Science—
describes in great detail three approaches to teaching science:

1. The morphological approach, or the process of
   generating ideas by analyzing the components of a
   system (phenomenon, activity). Using this approach, the
   teacher reflects on variables and generates questions,
   which, in turn, set the stage for experimentation.
2. The process approach, which is rooted in the processes
   of science, is the way the mind is engaged in understanding science. The author states that there can be no
   experimentation without the process of science and
   documents every aspect of the process, from observation
   to experimentation.

3. The ideation/generation approach, or brainstorming, is suggested as a creative way to think about science. It combines the first and second approaches and extends scientific experimentation to encompass human creativity. Using Frisbees as an example explains this approach further.

Section III addresses the thinking processes that are enhanced during science instruction. Creativity is the centerpiece of this section. Questioning as the key to problem solving is also presented, along with valuable instructional models.

Other topics include Science for the Gifted, Umbrellic Science Models, Spatial Development, and other provocative issues related to thinking and learning about science.

Section IV—Discrepant Events, Puzzles and Problems, and Tenacious Think Abouts—is an innovative approach that is hard to describe. It presents many useful tips on instruction to motivate children and engage them in scientific experimentation.

Dr. DeVito is an outstanding science educator because of his humorous, affective approach to science, which befriends teachers and stimulates them to help children engage in science and differentiates approaches that are appropriate for teaching children in primary and elementary classes.

DeVito, Alfred, and Gerald Krockover. *Creative Sciencing—A Practical Approach.* 2nd ed. Boston, Mass.: Little, Brown, 1980.

This book is concerned with creative methods of teaching science. The book is divided into six chapters with titles that suggest the immediacy of the topic. Chapter One, "Setting the Stage," addresses teachers' attitudes toward science and gives an overview of teaching methods that incorporate these attitudes. At times, the style is anecdotal, which helps to identify the authors' viewpoints. Chapter Two presents the conditions for creative science teaching, which presuppose flexibility, openness to individual interests and differences, good questioning strategies, and receptiveness to new technology, e.g., computers. Chapter Three addresses curriculum and emphasizes the integration of process skills and content, using a variety of strategies and materials. Chapter Four encourages teachers to incorporate other subjects to revise teaching, and Chapter Five confronts the logistics of daily teaching, including how to organize activities, where to order materials, safety, field trips, and special education. Finally, Chapter Six explores creative strategies for evaluations. The authors pause for questions to the reader and provoke thinking on how to involve children in the scientific process. Each chapter ends with a summary that helps to focus on the issues. This book is accompanied by "Creative Sciencing Ideas and Activities for Teachers and Children."

Diamond, Dorothy. *Introduction and Guide to Teaching Primary Science*. Milwaukee, Wis.: MacDonald-Raintree, 1979.

This book was written as an introduction to the ten books of the Macdonald Educational Series, begun in Great Britain as a project sponsored jointly by the Nuffield Foundation and the Social Science Research Council. It aims to assist non-science teachers with concrete suggestions on how to explore science teaching. The author encourages an interactive-integrative approach, in which children are involved at their own cognitive and interest levels. Although it is not a how-to book, it offers suggestions for activities, materials, and environments. Most of all it encourages teachers to encourage children in a wide range of interesting experiences that will help them develop investigative skills utilizing a variety of resources (books, materials, media, and the environment at large). This book will be most helpful to the teacher who is preparing to use any of the Macdonald series books for science teaching.

Doris, Ellen. *Doing What Scientists Do.* Portsmouth, N.H.: Heinemann, 1991.

Several assumptions frame this book:

1. Children learn best through hands-on experiences.
2. Children construct their own knowledge as they actively engage in learning.
3. Children's developmental levels influence how they feel about things, as well as their concepts.
4. The teacher plays a major role in how effectively children learn science.

The book engages the reader in creating and teaching science to young children in a concrete way. The chapters are organized as follows: Beginning Creating an Environment for Science in the Classroom, The First Class Meeting: What Do Scientists Do?, Children's First Work Period, Another Science Meeting, Sharing Work, Extending Science Work, Teacher as Facilitator, Interpreting Children's Work, Field Trips, Making Changes, and appendixes that contain worksheets that reflect children's scientific thinking.

A "how-to" book to engage teachers in a child-centered approach to teaching. The anecdotal content and suggestions presented in each chapter encourage and empower teachers to teach science in developmentally appropriate ways, which, in turn, empower children to learn to investigate their world "as scientists do."

Druger, Marvin (Ed.). *Science for the Fun of It.* Washington, D.C.: National Science Teachers Association, 1988.

This is a guide to informal science education. Obviously, children are exposed to science beyond the classroom, and the contributors to this publication highlight the out-of-school opportunities for learning science. The areas presented are the media—all the current viable programs, most of which are produced by Public Television stations; the museums and zoos—well known for their programs in science and important contributions to science education; and projects, competitions, and family activities—a wide variety of opportunities to get involved in science learning, including programs across the country that engage families and children in learning about science.

This is a useful reference book for all who are involved in the education of young children.

Duckworth, Eleanor. *The Having of Wonderful Ideas.* New York: Teachers College Press, 1987.

This book is a first-hand experience of the making of a "true" teacher. The chapters are valuable vignettes from the author's lifetime experiences in education and her connections with science.

Chapter 1 introduces such concepts as the role of learners in constructing their own knowledge, reflections on curriculum and subsequent evaluations, and how these concepts influence reform in teacher education.

Chapters 2 and 3 describe situations in the author's life when the issue was of learners constructing their own knowledge in relation to English. Chapter 3 discusses misconceptions on how to utilize Piaget's findings, as well as how to think about what is important in intellectual development.

Chapters 4 and 5 address issues of evaluation and how they are related to the goals of learning. Concrete episodes highlight the differences among evaluation systems and how they relate to teacher education.

Chapter 6 is a concrete account of the importance of learning in breadth and depth.

Chapters 7 and 8 focus on Piaget's work as it is perceived by teachers and its implications for how teachers acknowledge children's thinking.

Chapter 9—the aftermath of the training period—is a reflection on teachers' and children's thoughts and feelings about learning. The account starts with Robert Oppenheimer and the conflict between the person and his or her achievements.

In Chapter 10 the author presents her research on teaching and learning. She documents the learning process through which teachers go to construct their own knowledge of phenomena and how this understanding helps teachers' research on their students' learning processes.

The effectiveness of this publication lies in the author's skills in engaging the reader in a personal journey of teaching— and learning.

Duckworth, Eleanor, Jack Easley, David Hawkins, and Androula Henriques. *Science Education: A Minds-on Approach for the Elementary Years.* Hillsdale, N.J.: Lawrence Erlbaum Associates, 1990.

There are many questions concerning science education in the elementary grades: What is science? How do children engage in learning? How does science relate to the rest of the curriculum? What is the teacher's role?

The authors, well known in the field of science and education, base their views on these issues on the following assumptions: Science is a human activity that becomes meaningful when scientists think about and communicate science while they go about their scientific work. Learning occurs when the individual is actively involved in exploring, thinking, and constructing knowledge. The teacher shares these assumptions and, in turn, supports the children's ways of constructing knowledge; provides environments and materials that are part of the children's worlds of nature; and respects the children's findings and questions regardless of their age and development.

As Hawkins notes (p. 100), "a great deal of scientific discovery has come, and for children or adults can come from a curiosity that focuses on rather everyday phenomena, but that does so with a refinement of discrimination that our normal working routines do not involve."

These views are not part of the mainstream school culture, but are consistent with research on how children and adults learn effectively as they construct their own knowledge.

The paradigms and the authors' documented teaching experiences with teachers and children convincingly support their views.

Educational Development Corporation. *The ESS Reader.* Newton, Mass.: Educational Development Corporation, 1970.

This book discusses the rationale for the development of the Elementary Science Study Curriculum. The contributors to this reader support the active involvement of children in their learning of science and respect children's findings. Their philosophy on teaching shaped the ESS (Elementary Science Study) Program and the articles remain classics in the literature of how children learn effectively from their environment. Teachers with child-centered approaches to teaching will find these articles inspirational and supportive of an active science teaching approach.

Edwards, Clifford, and Robert L. Fisher. *Teaching Elementary School Science: A Competency Based Approach.* New York: Praeger, 1977.

The book's outstanding feature is its organization of what a teacher must know in order to teach elementary school science. The authors represent a competency based teaching view and provide a wide range of viewpoints on learning theories, behavioral objectives, teaching strategies, content organization, process skills, and evaluation techniques. The book includes a chapter on teaching simulation. Preservice and inservice teachers will want to utilize the exercises provided in the book for self-evaluation. It is a book that concerns itself more with *how* to teach than *what* to teach.

Esler, William K., and Mary K. Esler. *Teaching Elementary Science*. 3rd ed. Belmont, Calif.: Wadsworth, 1981.

A book on elementary school science that can be a textbook for teachers on "what" and "how" to teach science to children. Section One includes conceptual frameworks from all the areas that contribute to effective science teaching, i.e., children's levels of cognitive development (Piaget); behavior learning levels (Gagne); methods of sequencing the inquiry process as well as the content of science; strategies on how to integrate science with other subjects; curriculum theory; criteria on how to choose programs and textbooks, followed by brief descriptions of the well-known funded programs of the NSF.

Gega, Peter C. *Science in Elementary Education*. 4th ed. New York: Wiley, 1982.

This book helps teachers to understand the subject matter, develop science concepts from phenomena and materials around them, and plan strategies to teach these concepts to children. The first part of the book addresses issues such as children's learning, inquiry and science teaching, open and closed activities, resources for science teaching, mainstreaming special students, learning centers, and evaluation models. The second and lengthier part concentrates on the content of science and on strategies for teaching it to children. It differentiates between activities and investigations, incorporating problem solving with the latter.

The book is lively and rich in illustrations and diagrams. At the end of each chapter is a listing of appropriate trade books, differentiated by topic and grade level. The book contains a thorough professional bibliography and a special section on animal requirements for survival in science centers. Both preservice and inservice teachers will find this book most helpful because it offers valuable information on science for them as well as for children.

George, Kenneth D., Maureen Dietz, Eugene C. Abraham, and
    Miles A. Nelson. *Elementary School Science: Why and How.*
    Lexington, Mass.: Heath, 1974.

The book views the teaching of science as a decision-
making process. The decisions concern curricular, instructional, and evaluation issues. In the curricular part of the book,
the critical factors that influence decisions are learners'
developmental stages and the nature of the science program.
The instructional issues involve teaching tactics and strategies
for which the authors offer helpful explanations and examples.
Models of different teaching tactics (initiating, focusing, ter-
minating) are clearly stated. Strategies are considered as
choices teachers make to achieve an objective while they utilize
certain tactics. Finally, decisions on evaluation are discussed.
This book contributes greatly to the understanding of the
teaching process and offers guidelines to preservice and
inservice teachers on how to structure lessons and programs in
science.

Goldberg, Lazer. *Children and Science.* New York: Scribner's,
    1970.

This book aims to sensitize adults to the value of science
education for children. It addresses parents and teachers and
promotes the notion that science education is not a separate
entity, but must be integrated into the children's environment
wherever they are engaged in learning. Dr. Goldberg discusses
the value of science education as a contributor to the development of children's thinking processes and provides many
suggestions for adults (teachers, parents) on how to enhance
the values of this education. Finally, the author warns that
testing is a contradiction of the very goals of the philosophy of
science learning. The bibliography offers a wide selection of
works for children and adults that reinforce his viewpoints.

A very inspiring book for adults who are concerned that
children understand and appreciate science.

Good, Ronald G. *How Children Learn Science: Conceptual Development and Implications for Teaching*. New York: Macmillan, 1977.

This book models science teaching on Piagetian developmental theory. Concept development in science is related to the developmental stages of children and their notions of causality. The experimental interview is recommended as an effective strategy to determine a child's cognitive level and his understanding about causality in physical phenomena. Obviously, such an outlook has implications for a science curriculum, and concrete investigations are presented for various developmental stages, designating expected learning outcomes.

This is not a "how to teach" book, but one that utilizes research findings on Piagetian theory and children's thinking and develops a methodology for science teaching. Teachers will find this book very challenging in its approach to cognitive development and children's notions of causality, how such notions differ from one age to another, and what implications they have for science activities. Parts 4 and 6 respectively present science concepts and children's thinking at different levels, and ideas that help children learn science. Documented research findings throughout the book strengthen the position of the author.

Harlan, Jean. *Science Experiences for the Early Childhood Years*. 3rd ed. Columbus, Ohio: Merrill, 1983.

The rationale of this book lies in the assumption that young children's natural interest in knowing the physical world around them motivates them to engage in meaningful science experiences. This rationale helps teachers to plan and teach science to young children. Throughout the book, the science concepts to be taught are followed by planned activities— experiences for children that are enhanced by suggested integrative activities from the areas of art, math, body movement, music, and social studies. This method encourages teachers who may not feel comfortable with science to get involved through other topics where they may feel more comfortable. The topics explored include plant life, animal life, the human body, care and nourishment, air, water, seasons and weather, rocks and minerals, magnets, simple machines, sound, light, and electricity. Appendixes I and II offer references to music, poetry, body movement, and science materials. Each topic is accompanied by a valuable bibliography of related children's books and extensive reading for teachers.

Harlen, Wynne. (ed.). *Primary Science: Taking the Plunge.* London, England: Heinemann Press, 1985.

This widely known author on science education, along with four other authors, addresses all the issues involved in teaching elementary science.

Science for children is discussed, including process skills, the content, and their relationships to the curriculum. The importance of observation as an initiation to scientific investigations is highlighted. The art of questioning to stimulate children's thinking, as well as to help children to develop their own questioning skills, which leads them to problem solving, is discussed. Children's views of the world around them and the role of scientific investigations in validating or changing these views are examined.

A careful analysis is included of how children communicate their findings—writing, talking, drawing, modeling—all of which can be used to record the skills of science.

The writings in this book are inviting to those who teach science to young children. The authors involve readers in thinking about planning, as well as the actual teaching process, and encourage them to make decisions on how to apply the information in their unique situations. Excellent anecdotes also contribute to the success of this book.

Harlen, Wynne, and Sheila Jelly. *Developing Science in the Primary Classroom.* Portsmouth, N.H.: Heinemann, 1989.

This book combines the theoretical constructs on what is science and technology and how children learn with detailed strategies for practice.

The Foreword states that "Development is the theme of the book," and this theme evolves throughout the text. The teacher who wants to be in charge of her or his teaching practices will find this book extremely helpful.

The titles of the chapters give a hint of the clarity and purposefulness with which they were written: The Word "Science," Making a Start, How Are We Doing?, Developing the Work, Getting Ideas, Developing the Work, Curriculum and Classroom Organization, Where Are We Going? Development and Learning, and Development and Teaching Science.

Each chapter presents a combination of questions, diagrams, photographs, and narrative that take a wide perspective on how to teach science in relation to each teacher's individual classroom. They address developmental differences and connect science with the rest of the curriculum. All in 71 pages!

In addition to a selection of publications in primary science and technology, the four appendixes contain discussions on the following topics:

1. Process skills, attitudes, and concepts.
2. Learning in science in the primary grades.
3. Handling children's questions.
4. Safety in primary science.

Hausman, Howard Y. *Choosing a Science Program for the Elementary School.* Washington, D.C.: Council for Basic Education, 1976.

This monograph states the case for science education in elementary schools. The author offers examples from a wide selection of textbooks based on teaching and hands-on experience in science and discusses their differences. The NSF-funded science programs (ESS, S-APA, SCIS, COPES, Minnemast) are discussed as the hands-on science programs, and the importance of inservice teacher training for effective implementation is emphasized. A concise document with essential information for school administrators who decide on science programs for the elementary school.

Henson, Kenneth T., and Yank Delman. *Elementary Science Methods.* New York: McGraw-Hill, 1984.

The authors aim to acquaint teachers with "everything" that is involved in teaching science to children in elementary school. The book is useful as a reference for teachers in elementary school science. Part I discusses issues that relate to science teaching, i.e., why science for children; the nature of science; theories that contribute to our understanding of children's learning; theories on the planning and implementing of science teaching; and writing, objectives, and the evaluation of children's performance. Chapters 7 and 8 are particularly useful for their wide variety of resources and suggestions for the actual practice of science teaching and the integration of other curriculum areas (such as math and art) into science activities. Parts II, III, and IV are science content sections on life, earth, and physical science respectively. These sections include activities grouped for primary and intermediate grades.

Each chapter is well organized, but highly concentrated in concepts for the novice in science teaching. The rich range of suggested resources at the end of each chapter can contribute to the development of a library of children's and teachers' books that will enhance the teaching of science.

Hochman, Vivienne, and Mildred Greenwald. *Science Experiences in Early Childhood Education.* 6th ed. New York: Bank Street Publications, 1969.

This book on science for preschool children continues to be correct in its assumptions on how young children learn science and what are appropriate materials and strategies to enhance such learning. The focus is on young children's science experiences, rather than on experiments. The book offers a wide variety of suggested activities that can be integrated into children's lives, providing dynamic growth. At present, most preschool programs incorporate such strategies in teaching science to children, so this book continues to be valuable for teachers and parents of preschool children.

Holt, Bess, and Gene Holt. *Science with Young Children.* Washington, D.C.: N.A.E.Y.C., 1977.

This is a comprehensive book on how young children learn in science. It discusses the broad role of science in the development of the child, relates the process skills of science to children's investigative capabilities, and identifies children's natural curiosity as a motivating force for the exploration of materials and phenomena. The author offers concrete suggestions to teachers on how to develop environments, suggest activities, and guide experiences in science for children. At all times the planning of science activities takes into account children's developmental needs. The element of safety in teaching science is discussed and the valuable appendix on common poisonous plants should be in everybody's possession, especially those who take nature walks with children.

Humphrey, James H. *Teaching Elementary Science Through Motor Learning.* Springfield, Ill.: Thomas, 1975.

Science education through motor activity is one theory on how to teach science concepts effectively to children in the elementary grades. The author explains the nature of physical education activities and their importance to concept learning. He claims support for his views from historical sources, which range from Plato (380 B.C.) to L.P. Jacks (1932). There are lesson plans that illustrate how science concepts can be played out through motor activities, and the author emphasizes their particular value for slow learners. Teaching science through motor learning should not be confused with active learning in science, which is a widely accepted format in the teaching of science concepts. For example, in teaching the concept that "electricity is the flow of electrons in a closed circuit" through motor learning strategies, the children simulate the closed circuit with their bodies and use a ball to represent the current of flow of electrons. On the other hand, in an environment where active learning takes place, the children may use batteries and bulbs to understand the closed circuit concept.

Hurd, Paul Dehart, and James J. Gallagher. *New Directions in Elementary Science Teaching.* Belmont, Calif.: Wadsworth, 1968.

The focus of this book is descriptions of 13 elementary science programs funded by the NSF, the U.S. Office of Education, and several private foundations. The programs described include COPES, S-APA, ESSP (Berkeley), ESSP (Illinois), ESSP (Utah State), ESS, IDP, ISCS, Minnemast, SSCP, SCIS, SQAIESS, and WIMSA. Each program is described in a comprehensive manner and includes instructional materials, desirable learning outcomes, sample lessons, and conditions for successful implementation. The book is a valuable reference for teachers (preservice and inservice) and school admini-strators, and a note to parents further expands its usefulness. The appendixes provide reference information and addresses for each program.

Ivany, J.W. George. *Today's Science; A Professional Approach to Teaching Elementary School Science.* Chicago: Science Research Associates, 1975.

Professionalism in the teaching of science has a special meaning in this book. The author equates professionalism with decision-making and eclecticism on the "whats" and "hows" of teaching science to children. The emergence of professionalism in science teaching has to do with pedagogical methods, "flexibility in style," and a personal philosophy based on sound concepts of science and the nature of learning. Each chapter addresses an issue that relates to the teaching of science (nature of science, children, learning models of teaching, and more) and concludes with a summary of the key concepts discussed and a series of exercises testing the teacher's capabilities in decision-making on the issues discussed. The style is direct and concise and the arguments on professionalism for teachers are consistent throughout the text. The author exhibits the same openness to other views and sustains an unbiased viewpoint in the decision-making exercises. The book will interest teachers and school administrators as a model for decision-making and in choosing a curriculum in science.

Jacobson, Willard, and Abby Baroy Bergman. *Science for Children: A Book for Teachers*. Englewood Cliffs, N.J.: Prentice Hall, 1980.

The authors present a comprehensive view of teaching for preservice and inservice teachers in elementary science education. In Part I they support the views that science teaching for children must go beyond the classroom and become part of their daily lives. They discuss extensively how teaching science can help children in perceptual development, logical and formal thinking, language skills, and math development. It can also offer special benefits to the handicapped. The role of the teacher is emphasized throughout the book and a competency-based teacher education program in elementary school science is organized in the Appendix. Part II presents science background for the teacher so that the activities suggested will reflect teacher understanding of both the content and the process of science. An extensive bibliography follows each chapter, and services are classified for teachers and for younger and older children.

Jacobson, Willard J., and Harold E. Tannebaum. *Modern Elementary School Science: A Recommended Sequence.* New York: Columbia University Press, 1961.

The authors respond to the question, "What is science?" in terms of the elementary school. They recommend a two-dimensional program: a "flexible dimension" that relates science to everyday life and other subjects of the curriculum, and a "planned dimension" where high-quality experiences in science are proposed as part of the science program. The recommended sequence in planning a science program is the focal point of the book. The authors take into consideration goals, characteristics, and criteria for planning a program. They suggest that content areas from all fields of science offer strategies in the organization and teaching of the program. They further propose materials and facilities and expand on evaluation guidelines. This book is a forerunner of later books on the planning of science programs in the elementary schools.

Kambly, Paul E., and John E. Suttle. *Teaching Elementary School Science Methods and Resources.* New York: The Ronald Press, 1963.

This book utilizes a traditional methods approach and represents the attitudes and science teaching styles that prevailed prior to the 1960s. It is precise, filled with valuable science information, and can be used as a resource by teachers who may want additional ideas on initiating and developing field, experimental, and culminating activities in various areas of science.

Karplus, Robert, and Herbert D. Thier. *A New Look at Elementary School Science.* Chicago: Rand McNally, 1967.

A most valuable book for users of the SCIS curriculum in elementary science. It offers a historical sequence of the development of the project, incorporates the new visions in science teaching that the program reflects, and is useful to students in science education who wish to learn about the exemplary elementary science programs of the 1960s and their part in the teaching of science to children. The book offers no frills in appearance, but it is a classic in content.

Kuslan, Louis I., and Harris A. Stone. *Readings on Teaching Children Science*. Belmont, Calif.: Wadsworth, 1969.

This book incorporates a wide range of viewpoints on elementary science for children. Thirty-nine articles fall into the categories of goals of science, natures of science and children, curriculum objectives and instructional strategies, evaluation, models in teacher preparation and teaching science to children. The contributors are well known in the fields of child development, curriculum, and science education. Most of the articles document research and findings that clarify many assumptions made on the teaching of science to children. The style varies, but the articles are brief and focused and present assumptions, data, and conclusions on science teaching that will interest administrators and teachers of science in elementary schools.

Kuslan, Louis I., and Harris A. Stone. *Teaching Children Science: An Inquiry Approach*. Belmont, Calif.: Wadsworth, 1968.

This book introduces the reader to the history of inquiry teaching. It offers a historical overview (100 years of elementary school science) which is a welcome addition to the evaluation of the inquiry process in teaching science. It includes all the well-known elementary science programs of the 1960s and discusses a wide range of factors that contribute to effective inquiry-based teaching. However, the book is not helpful to newcomers in science teaching, because it is only toward the end that the authors offer application of inquiry teaching through actual science experiments.

Landsdowne, Brenda, Paul Blackwood, and Paul Brandwein. *Teaching Elementary Science Through Investigation and Colloquium.* New York: Harcourt Brace Jovanovich, 1971.

This book presents one of the most comprehensive analyses of the inquiry method in science teaching. The authors succeed in interweaving theory and practice through examples that include conversations between teachers and children during actual science teaching. Inquiry in teaching science responds to children's developmental needs and encourages involvement at all stages. Materials play a major role and children "mess around" during initial discoveries and then are encouraged to discuss their findings, which in turn contributes to concept development. The teacher is a key factor through the entire process and evaluation is ongoing and systematic, based on observation techniques and not on pencil and paper tests. Furthermore, structured textbook science programs that dictate objectives and goals in science learning are viewed unfavorably. Teachers and administrators will find strong arguments in this book in favor of a more open-discovery colloquium method for teaching science to children.

Lewis, Jane E., and Irene C. Potter. *The Teaching of Science in the Elementary School.* 2nd ed. Englewood Cliffs, N.J.: Prentice Hall, 1970.

In this book, the goal of science teaching is the practice of process skills which lead to the understanding of the content of science. Some helpful suggestions are offered on how to integrate science in other areas of the curriculum and how to order materials for a science program. The major part of the book is devoted to the content of science (earth, physical, life sciences). Chapters 6 through 48 are organized theoretically and in conceptual frameworks. Each chapter includes leading questions that encourage the practice of process skills. The book is rich in science concepts and investigations and teachers with some science background will appreciate it even more than those without. The book is interjected with topics on technology and encourages scientific investigation on subjects like radioactivity and space flight. Although several investigations are appropriate for young children (6 to 8), the focus of the teaching is the higher elementary grades.

Lind, Karen K. *Exploring Science in Early Childhood—A Developmental Approach*. Albany, N.Y.: Delmar Publishers, 1991.

A developmental approach to involving children in learning science, written for students in training and teachers in early childhood education.

The book is divided into four sections. Section I expands on concept development—how it applies to science, how children's concept building varies through their development, how assessment reflects their learning. A wide range of examples are presented to demonstrate planning and concept building in science.

Section II goes further in describing the learning of skills and concepts related to science. Scientific and math skills are discussed in theory and applied in practice through a wide selection of appropriate activities.

Section III focuses on a science curriculum for young children that is closely related to their everyday life and emphasizes that the children's use of their senses is essential to their explorations. Life sciences include plants and animals. Physical science features bubbles, kites and parachutes, bottles and water. Earth science focuses on rocks in various forms; i.e., pebbles, ice, cookies, crystal making, and so forth. Finally, the chapter on health and nutrition examines foods and their contribution to well-being concretely and in interrelated ways.

Section IV focuses on the environment where science takes place: how to set up a learning center and science in the home. Developmental assessment tasks conclude this usable book.

The format is very approachable and appropriate to beginning science teachers. Thematic webs and suggested resources contribute to the scope of these topics.

The book could also be used as a text for students in early childhood education on how to teach developmentally appropriate science to young children.

Link, Michael. *Outdoor Education*. Englewood Cliffs, N.J.: Prentice Hall, 1981.

This book is a primer for teachers who want to get involved in outdoor education.

It is organized in 12 chapters: Outdoor Inspiration, Who Are You Going to Teach?, What to Expect, Activities for Class and Community, Outdoor Activities, Writing Your Own Unit, Your Local Nature Center, Workshops for Teachers, Spirals, Bad Weather and Fears, Tread Lightly, and Expedition Planning.

The content ranges from lists on how to plan a field trip, to science-based do's and don'ts on topics to be encountered outdoors, to developmentally differentiated pedagogy, to adjusting learning outcomes for children with special needs.

It will contribute to a science program that encourages hands-on, experiential involvement in learning about the environment. The content is enhanced with lists of appropriate questions, photography, and facts related to science and the environment.

Loucks-Horsley, Susan et al. *Elementary School Science for the 90s*. Alexandria, VA: A.S.C.D., 1990.

Learning about science has become necessary for our survival. Citizens who are well informed about science and technology are essential if we are to make the right decisions on the welfare of our planet. That is the rationale behind this book. It has been written for decision makers who have to share responsibility for science programs.

The chapters address questions that emerged from the 13 findings of the National Center for Improving Science Education:

1. Make science basic.
2. Build a curriculum that nurtures conceptual understanding.
3. Connect science to technology.
4. Include scientific attitudes and skills as important goals.
5. View science learning from a constructivist perspective.
6. Use a constructivist-oriented instructional model to guide learning.
7. Assess what is valued.
8. Connect curriculum, instruction, and assessment.
9. Use a variety of assessment strategies.
10. Assess programs as well as students.
11. View teachers' development as a continuous process.
12. Choose effective approaches to staff development.
13. Provide teachers with adequate support to implement good science programs.

Each chapter addresses one of these recommendations and informs the reader about what is known, what can be done, and what roles can be played by the various levels of leadership in designing the curriculum of science. Exemplary practices and key references are included.

A comprehensive study of the recommended course of action for planning and disseminating science education in the elementary grades to meet the needs of the next century.

McIntyre, Margaret. *Early Childhood and Science: A Collection of Articles Reprinted from Science and Children.* Washington, D.C., N.S.T.A., 1984.

A book that addresses the increasing demands for preschool science. It represents a wide documentation of work with young children and science and includes articles on how children learn, teaching strategies, and practical experiences with children. It is of special interest to teachers and parents of young children. Indeed, a much needed and welcome contribution to early childhood education.

National Science Resources Center. *Science for Children: Resources for Teachers.* Washington, D.C.: National Academy Press, 1988.

Although this book belongs in a category of its own, it is presented in this section as a generic resource for teachers that parallels the present publication but goes beyond the scope of this book.

A truly comprehensive resource guide for planners, science coordinators, and school or museum personnel who work on science education. A wide selection of scientists and educators contributed to the compilation of these resources.

The book is based on the assumption that science is learned through hands-on experimentation with developmentally appropriate expectations. The students experiment, ask questions, find their own answers, and probe problems all through their learning.

The book is organized in three sections. Section I includes curriculum materials—teachers' guides and activity packets, as well as kits and equipment that engage elementary-age children in hands-on science activities. The categories covered are life science, health and human biology, earth science, physical science, and multidisciplinary and applied science.

Section II includes activity books that further enhance hands-on science.

Section III includes lists of books on teaching science, science books, other references, and magazines for children and teachers.

It also presents an exhaustive list of museums, associations, publishers, and suppliers who are resources of programs and materials on science education.

Several indexes are organized to serve the reader. The entries are grouped by topic, title, author-project, grade level, and sources of information and assistance.

A truly valuable reference book at a reasonable price ($7.95) for everyone who is involved in science education.

Navarra, John Gabriel, and Joseph Zaffaroni. *Science in the Elementary School: Content and Methods*. Columbus, Ohio: Merrill, 1975.

The authors employ the inquiry method to help the reader investigate the content of their work. The first part of the book examines the meaning of science in elementary education and states guidelines for curriculum, resources, and strategies for teaching. The remaining and longer part offers a broad spectrum of science and teaching suggestions. The areas of science are organized into the following categories: (1) air-weather-flight, (2) space-time and earth, and (3) matter-energy-life. Each chapter states its objectives for what content must be learned and is followed by a section with more objectives for how to teach it to children. The teaching objectives incorporate process skills, discussion, field trips, and other curriculum areas where necessary. The book is a valuable reference for teachers who feel comfortable with science and the inquiry process.

Neugebauer, Bonnie (Ed.). *The Wonder of It: Exploring How the World Works*. Redmond, Wash.: Exchange Press, 1989.

The contributors to this book understand how young children learn, what science is, and how important a role science plays in the lives of children. Science is a natural, human activity that springs from the innate curiosity of children (and adults), engages them in hands-on explorations, and contributes to their understanding of the world.

The book is divided into three sections: Sharing the Wonder—Teachers and Children Together, Seeing Possibilities Everywhere—Ideas for Science Learning, and Nurturing a Global Perspective. Written in an informal, enthusiastic style, the chapters within each section are inspirational. The content relates to the practice of teaching science within a theoretical framework and reflects an integrative approach in teaching science based on hands-on experiences from the daily lives of children. Concrete recommendations are offered, such as how to set up science centers in the classroom, the role of questioning, discovering our bodies, and learning science from our pets.

The bibliographies are very useful and include lists of practical resources, such as catalogues, magazines, and professional organizations. This book is a valuable companion to the teacher of young children who is beginning to incorporate science into her or his curriculum in a developmentally appropriate way.

Osborne, Roger, and Peter Freyberg. *Learning in Science: Implications of Children's Science.* Portsmouth, N.H.: Heinemann Press, 1985.

The authors' views on children learning science are based on assumptions derived from developmental theories on how children construct knowledge about their world. This concrete, experiential approach is the cornerstone of the science teaching and learning sequence featured in this book.

The book is organized in five parts: (1) The Problem, (2) Towards Specific Solutions, (3) Wider Considerations, (4) Towards a Teaching Model, and (5) Implications for Curriculum and Teacher Education.

In Part 1, the authors discuss children's views of the world, how adults fail to understand these views, and the implications for science teaching. Part 2 explores in detail, and provides examples of, children's understanding in science and how teaching science to young children should build on this understanding. An activity-based approach to science teaching supports children's modes of learning and, as research has shown, is most successful.

Part 3 includes a substantive chapter on the important role of the teacher in science education. Part 4 examines teaching models and consolidates findings from research. The recommended model is exemplified through methods of teaching older children about electric currents. Part 5 examines the implications of science in the curriculum. Using the results of their research, the authors document and describe in detail the similar pedagogical problems that arise in other subjects.

The appendixes provide the research tools used by the authors and explicitly and realistically discuss how children's thinking and learning may be assessed.

Pitz, Albert, and Robert Sund. *Creative Teaching of Science in the Elementary School.* Boston, Mass.: Allyn and Bacon, 1974.

The authors present an overview of the history of science education and argue that present science teaching will become more effective if elements of creativity are incorporated in curricula and strategies. This approach offers a great opportunity for teachers and children to "unleash their creative abilities and become richer individuals." Science beyond the classroom—at home, in museums, or in libraries—is discussed. Studying the lives and works of well-known scientists also contributes to creative science learning. The curriculum reform of the 1960s is reviewed as it relates to the role of creativity and concrete examples clarify and demonstrate this point of view. The style is enthusiastic, inspirational, and convincing, and a selective bibliography on creativity encourages teachers to read further.

Raper, George, and John Stringer. *Encouraging Primary Science.* Philadelphia, Pa.: Cassell Publishers, 1987.

In defining science education, assumptions about children's learning, and the process of implementing a science curriculum, the authors have undertaken a major task. In this book, they include every aspect of planning and teaching science in the classroom, and provide a systematic sequence and examples of how to think about the nature and context of primary science.

Children's thinking as it relates to science is demonstrated through incidental conversations with children reported in Chapter 2. Chapters 3, 4, and 5 focus on policy issues related to how science can become a viable curriculum in schools. Problems hindering science education are identified and solutions for teachers and principals provided, including the recommendation that science curriculum developers and coordinators should be added to the staff.

Chapters 6 and 7 address the actual process of teaching and learning in science. The charts, diagrams, and strategies on science topics offer many concrete implementation paradigms. Chapter 8 provides practical suggestions to help teachers overcome any organizational difficulties they may encounter. Chapter 9, Practicalities, includes all other topics that were not discussed elsewhere in the book—from safety issues, to storage, to the care of animals and plants in the school, to resources for teachers to enhance their own understanding and provide ideas on science teaching.

Appendixes I and II contain examples of content guidelines for various age groups and concepts. Appendix III lists recommended guides for teaching science.

This 175-page resource should inspire educators to engage in the planning and implementation of a science program for the primary and elementary grades.

Renner, John W., and William Ragan. *Teaching Science in the Elementary School*. New York: Harper & Row, 1968.

The authors support the idea that children's developmental stages determine the learning of concepts and claim that an understanding of science is basic to children's ability to think. The book is unique in its modeling of science teaching on inquiry that combines process skills (observing, measuring, interpreting, and so forth) with essential concepts in science (matter, space, time, energy, and change). The NSF programs are discussed with reference to established criteria on the role of the teacher and learning environment and the book concludes with evaluation models. The appendixes are unique and include case studies of famous scientists, methods of organizing data collection, and a cognitive analysis for levels of thought. The book should be of great interest to experienced science educators and curriculum developers in general.

Roche, Ruth L. *The Child and Science: Wondering, Exploring, Growing.* Washington, D.C.: Association for Childhood Education International, 1977.

This monograph offers a convincing rationale for why young children should get involved in science. The author uses vignettes that describe both children's science experiences and the concept formations that children develop through these activities. This book will encourage any hesitant teacher of young children (preservice or inservice) to get involved in science teaching. It is brief, clear, and to the point and the inserted poetry makes it inspirational.

Romey, William D. *Confluent Education in Science.* New York: Ash Lad Press, 1976.

The term "confluent education" encompasses the affective as well as the cognitive aspects of education. In this case the term refers to the integration of language arts, humanities, etc., with science. The book offers examples of instances where "confluent" approaches maximize science learning and strengthen the assumption that motivation is directly linked to learning. Teachers will be encouraged to incorporate science into their overall curriculum. The style is clear, enthusiastic, and convincing.

Romey, William D. *Inquiry Techniques for Teaching Science.* Englewood Cliffs, N.J.: Prentice Hall, 1968.

This book is organized in two parts. The first part introduces the idea of the active learning of issues related to science teaching (concept formation, teaching strategies, inquiry) and the importance of developing a personal style of teaching. Each topic begins with an activity that involves the readers and follows with criteria that assist them in evaluating their responses. The second part of the book is comprised of articles from well-known scholars in the fields of learning, science education, curriculum development, and evaluation. The viewpoints presented reflect diversity. The book succeeds in challenging teachers of science to re-examine their teaching styles and/or develop new ones based on a better understanding of what teaching science to children is really all about.

Rowe, Mary Budd. *Teaching Science as a Continuous Inquiry: A Basic.* 2nd ed. New York: McGraw-Hill, 1978.

Science teaching is here viewed as synonymous with scientific literacy and relates to contemporary issues such as pollution, food, energy, etc. In the view of the author, science is basic and the implications of what students learn go beyond the level of factual knowledge to include language, logic development, and attitude formation. She makes strong arguments in favor of her philosophy. The writing combines an inquiry-based orientation with a humanistic style that includes a wide range of anecdotes that effectively connect theoretical constructs to practical learning. One example of such effort is Chapter 2, titled "Go Fly a Kite," which demonstrates how the experience of flying a kite can be planned and implemented to enlist a wide range of learning for children in all of the curriculum areas (language arts, math, art, science, social studies). The entire book emphasizes how science process skills and concepts are essential to science learning. The ways in which school environments and teacher roles can enhance inquiry-oriented science are discussed, and considerations are extended to management of group learning, logistics in using manipulators, variables for teaching the handicapped, and types of evaluation. Furthermore, the implications of science learning in the context of the problems of everyday living are recognized (ecological examination of populations, pollution). The book will spark the imagination of the teacher who wants to look at science teaching beyond the isolated lesson plans and the limits of the behavioral objectives that science curricula usually offer.

Sund, Robert B., and Roger W. Bybee. *Becoming a Better Elementary Science Teacher: A Reader.* Columbus, Ohio: Merrill, 1973.

The authors aim to expand teachers' capabilities beyond the teaching of the subject matter. They discuss issues of motivation and learning, special children, the art of questioning, all aspects of curriculum development, affective objectives, diverse views on evaluation, and the role of discovery and inquiry in science teaching. Teachers will find this reader helpful in developing their own viewpoints on how to teach science, as well as other subjects, effectively.

Thier, Herbert D. *Teaching Elementary School Science: A Laboratory Approach.* Lexington, Mass.: D.C. Heath, 1970.

A laboratory-centered approach to science teaching is the focal point of this book. The life sciences are organized as a study of organisms viewed in their complexity, organization, and interrelationships with their environments and the physical sciences as an explanation of matter—its structure and properties as part of a system, and energy as evidence of interaction with the system. These viewpoints are also reflected in the organization of SCIS (Science Curriculum Improvement Study) to whose development the author has contributed.

The author goes on to discuss learning from a developmental viewpoint, learning environments inside and outside the classroom, and the role of the teachers and evaluators.

A valuable book for preservice and inservice teachers, science curriculum developers, and most of all for users of the SCIS curriculum.

Trojcak, Doris A. *Science with Children.* New York: McGraw-Hill, 1979.

The author explains to teachers how to comprehend science, how to help children discover the wonders of the natural world, and how to develop the conditions so that both these things can occur. All this appears as a direct dialogue with teachers that presents to them a range of possibilities on how to sharpen their decision-making abilities through skills learned in science and how to adapt strategies to their styles of teaching. Part I explores science as content and process and discusses how it can be adapted to children's learning capabilities. Piaget's theories and tasks on conservation are discussed and illustrated in detail. Part II combines the teaching of science skills with child-centered elements. Many exemplary activities illustrate how this can occur. Part III challenges the teacher to utilize science skills to develop instructional strategies and implement science teaching. Finally, the teacher is shown how to analyze the existing science curricula—S-APA, SCIS, ESS—and evolve a philosophy and a course of action most appropriate to his own teaching style and to children's levels of development and interest. The book offers inspiration to preservice and inservice teachers to become thinkers and decision makers and not just consumers of existing curricula in science.

Vessel, M.F. *Elementary School Science Teaching.* Washington, D.C.: Center for Applied Research in Education, 1963.

This monograph focuses on issues in elementary school science in the early 1960s. The author develops a logical, historically aware sequence of arguments on the nature of science education and traces the making of science curriculum. The book concludes with a chapter on "Development and

Trends" that incorporates the "new" guidelines presented by the AAAS (American Association for the Advancement of Science). Professor Vessel offers an insight on how thinking in elementary science education began to change in the early 1960s.

Victor, Edward. *Science for the Elementary School.* 4th ed. New York: Macmillan, 1980.

This is a classic methods book in the teaching of elementary science. It is divided into two parts. Part I includes learning theories, children's developmental stages, and how they influence the teaching of science. Objectives in elementary science curricula and strategies for implementation are discussed. Important methodology in classroom teaching is presented and a wide range of sample teaching and resource units are offered, with an overview of possible materials to be used in the classroom. Evaluation models conclude the first part of the book. Part II, the largest section, focuses on the content of science and is divided into living things, earth, and physical sciences. Each chapter is followed by a list of appropriate activities and a bibliography. This mammoth favorite is in its fourth edition and will mainly interest preservice teachers who will appreciate a structured approach to the teaching of science, with a wide range of diagrams, drawings of materials, experiments, and helpful appendixes.

Victor, Edward, and Marjorie S. Lerner. *Readings in Science Education for the Elementary School.* 3rd ed. New York: Macmillan, 1975.

A comprehensive view of science education. The selected readings reflect the thinking of well-known writers in science education and related fields and represent a wide range of viewpoints. The book is divided into eight sections. The role of science in the elementary school appears in Section One, including a position statement on NSTA. Section Two explains theories of intellectual development and learning, featuring

Piaget, Bruner, and Gagne. A wide range of objectives in elementary science are discussed in Section Three. Elementary science programs are reviewed in Section Four. Section Five offers a variety of approaches to classroom teaching, including the development of questioning skills, team teaching, and the unit as a science teaching strategy. Section Six elaborates on evaluation, and Section Seven on the planning and creating of materials and facilities. The last section devotes considerable space to the training of science teachers and the role of administrators and science supervisors.

Washton, Nathan Seymour. *Teaching Science in Elementary and Middle Years*. New York: McKay, 1974.

The book offers guidelines on how to study science education for personal development and how to apply that learning in the teaching of science to children. Part I incorporates the components that prepare one for science teaching—philosophy, psychology methods of teaching—with a detailed analysis of objectives and macro/micro lesson planning, criteria for choosing science curricula, recommendations on how to teach individuals and groups, and instruction on how to incorporate evaluation. Part II details a chronological sequence in the teaching of science concepts from kindergarten to eighth grade. The remainder of the book explores the various categories of science: living, air, water, weather, earth, matter, energy, electricity, magnets, heat, sound, and light. The style is direct, precise, and traditional in its approach. It is exceptionally rich in activity ideas, and the differentiation of teaching methods for each grade level will be helpful to new teachers.

Wasserman, Selma, and J.W. George Ivany. *Teaching Elementary Science—Who's Afraid of Spiders?*. New York: Harper & Row, 1988.

The book aims to make science teaching a rewarding experience for teachers. The authors identify the two distinct ways in which science can be taught. They support and coin "sciencing" as the teaching strategy that involves the learner in the act of doing science and oppose the didactic textbook approach with teacher-directed activities. They claim the learning outcomes are very different for each approach. Their perspectives for appropriate classroom practices include principles of child development and perspectives on play, as well as on teaching for thinking. These practices can be achieved through the instructional model of play-debrief-replay.

The authors describe in detail how to involved children in doing science through play-debrief-replay. The organization of the book facilitates the implementation of this model. The chapters are: (1) Teachers, Children, and Science: Theoretical Perspectives, (2) Organizing the Science Program, (3) Thinking and Decision Making in Science, (4) 60 Sciencing Activities, and (5) Journey into the Unknown.

The science program is a result of a research project conducted by the authors and has been field tested in many classrooms. The informal, personal style conveys this message to make teachers of children "teachers of science without tears." Each of the 60 activities is organized in an exhaustive, detailed manner and illustrate very clearly the play-debrief-replay instructional model in teaching science to children.

Waters, Barbara. *Science Can Be Elementary: Discovery-Action Programs for K-3*. New York: Citation Press, 1973.

This book offers a comprehensive overview of the NSF-funded elementary science programs of the 1960s, i.e., ESS, SCIS, COPES, S-APA, and Minnemast. It examines them as they relate to concept building, process skills, and content, but most of all as they support child-centered approaches in teaching. The author favors a developmental-interaction approach to teaching and encourages teachers to use children's natural curiosity to get them involved in science, and to be open and flexible to outcomes. The author maintains an informal and direct style, provides teachers with science activities, and encourages them to get involved in science teaching. The Appendixes offer a wide selection of professional information on resources for teaching science, e.g., supplies, bibliography, and organizations.

III

Science Activities Books

Introduction

Science activities books are written primarily for the adults who engage children in science learning. Most authors assume a hands-on approach to science learning and encourage children's involvement. However, there is a considerable difference in pedagogy on how to teach science effectively to children that, in turn, influences learning outcomes. These differences are based on assumptions of how young children learn most effectively, whether science is taught as a process or with an emphasis on content, whether learning outcomes are prescribed by the teacher or are child-directed, and whether or not science activities are integrated in the curriculum of the early childhood program.

How Children Learn Science Effectively

One of the criteria used to evaluate the activities books is the author's perspective on how children learn science effectively. In general, the authors do not expand on learning theories and children's developmental stages, but some do suggest developmental guidelines on how to involve children in science learning while others do not. For example, in *Experiences in Science for Young Children* by Donald B. Neuman,[1] the author's guidelines on how to involve children in the activities are based on knowledge about child development and behavioral objectives. The author guides the educator through the thinking process of children and assists him or her in organizing the activities so children can adapt their learning according to their developmental stages and to well-defined objectives.

In other books, such as *Experiments with Everyday Objects: Science Activities for Children, Parents and Teachers* by Kevin Goldstein-Jackson,[2] the author does not base the activities upon developmental guidelines, but presents them with directions for what to do as children reach the desirable outcomes. They are more like recipes, with clearly stated learning outcomes, and do not indicate for which age group they would be most appropriate.

The majority of the books present an eclectic viewpoint, in which developmental differentiations determine a wide range of science activity.

Process vs. Content of Science

Another area in which science activity books differ is in how science ought to be organized for teaching purposes. Robert Gagne, who has influenced the organization of science materials for teaching, considers the process of scientific research essential to the teaching of science to children. This view influences the authors of many science activities books, while others focus their writing on the content of science.

In the books influenced by scientific inquiry, children confront problems and the authors assist them in finding solutions through the scientific method of observing, data collecting, communicating, manipulating objects, hypothesizing, and predicting. In the book *Science on a Shoestring* by Herb Strongin,[3] the emphasis is on the development of scientific skills as a way to understand the content of science. In one activity,[4] children study changes in the environment and rely completely on their skills of observation to collect data on how the shadow of the flag pole in the school yard moves through the day. On the basis of their data collecting, they will hypothesize on and infer the causes of this movement.

In contrast, other books choose content of science as their primary focus. Children engage in making things, probing objects, and learning about physical phenomena by following detailed instructions. One such book, rich in science content, is the all-time favorite *Sourcebook for Science Teaching* by UNESCO.[5] It is carefully constructed to contain activities from all areas of science and each activity demonstrates a concept, principle, or phenomenon. For example, a series of experiments is constructed to demonstrate how pumps use air pressure, while in another section simple experiments with everyday things illustrate static electricity. In both cases, instructions must be carefully followed so the desirable outcome will prevail.

Whose Learning Outcome?

Another criteria in the review of these books is the goals and objectives of the authors on what the learning outcomes should be. In a book such as the UNESCO *Sourcebook*, the authors state the learning outcomes for each activity; their goals are that children gain a wide variety of scientific knowledge about objects and phenomena. The authors provide instructions and illustrations so that children are assisted in doing a wide variety of experiments with well-defined, desirable outcomes. In other words, a successful conclusion of the experiment must coincide with the learning outcomes suggested in the book.

This approach is in contrast to other books' objectives, in which the activity itself is the goal and the learning outcomes are more child-defined. The authors of such books emphasize that the child's involvement in the activity be on his terms and not on preconceived learning directives and outcomes based on an adult's viewpoint. That is, a child's involvement in collecting seashells and grouping them in ways s/he feels they belong is more important than the knowledge of what kinds of seashells s/he brings back to the class. A child experiencing the wind through kite flying is more important than identifying the northwesterly direction of the wind and its speed. In *Sharing Nature with Children* by J.B. Cornell, the author suggests that children go "hiking" in the woods on their bellies holding a magnifying glass. He places the emphasis on learning outcomes that originate with children's interests, observations, and collections.

However, most of the books reflect a middle-of-the-road approach. The authors define the science content of the activities and introduce a strategy that facilitates the projected learning outcome, but encourage children to further probe the object or phenomena as their interests dictate.

Science, Part of or Separate from the Early Childhood Program K–3?

It is natural for children to seek knowledge and understanding of the world around them. The dilemma that exists is whether the knowledge and the process that produces it should permeate the entire learning experience of the child or whether it should be offered as a separate venture.

There are opposing views on this issue. One view is that the goal of science teaching is valuable learning and should be pursued for its own merit. Another belief holds that the kind of learning that is generated by science should serve as the backbone of the curriculum and be part of all the learning areas.

The controversy on this issue is a result of basic differences in pedagogy. The approach that would keep science a separate learning experience for young children is based on the assumption that scientific knowledge is important for its own sake. It is imperative that children's scientific literacy be treated separately so that children will develop mastery of skills and facts in science, such as knowing seashells, dissecting fish and learning their parts and functions, and so forth.

The other view is that effective learning for children occurs when children experience it as a part of their lives. For example, weather can be taught as part of the daily experience of living and not as an isolated lesson, and fish can be dissected as part of a continuous lifelong experience like visiting an aquarium, the fishmarket, or the beach; eating a fish; or reading a story about fish. Furthermore, the scientific process used to find out about things and phenomena is good pedagogy in itself and should permeate the entire curriculum of early childhood programs.

In *Creative Sciencing—A Practical Approach* by Alfred DeVito and Gerald Krockover,[6] the integration of the "spirit of science" into the total curriculum is regarded simply as good teaching. Observation, experimentation, questioning, analysis, and interpretation of data are significant tools for all areas of the curriculum.

In summary, the authors that focus on science activities represent a wide range of viewpoints, each with its own eclectic rationale.

NOTES

1. Neuman, Donald B. *Experiences in Science for Young Children.* Albany, N.Y.: Delmar, 1978.

2. Goldstein-Jackson, Kevin. *Experiments with Everyday Objects: Science Activities for Children, Parents and Teachers.* Englewood Cliffs, N.J.: Prentice Hall, 1978.

3. Strongin, Herb. *Science on a Shoestring.* Menlo Park, Calif.: Addison Wesley, 1976.

4. *Ibid.,* p. 46.

5. *UNESCO Sourcebook for Science Teaching.* Paris, France: UNESCO, 1962.

6. DeVito, Alfred, and Gerald Krockover. *Creative Sciencing—A Practical Approach.* Boston, Mass.: Little, Brown, 1976.

BIBLIOGRAPHY

Allison, Linda. *The Reasons for Seasons/Blood & Guts.* Boston,
    Mass.: Little, Brown/Yolla Bolly Press, 1975.

Two books from a series for children and adults written
together by a group of California writers, teachers, and artists.
They combine science concepts—the earth moves around the
sun, thus the reason for seasons—with activities that motivate
children to observe, get involved in the science aspects of the
seasons, and integrate them in their daily lives. For example,
under the topic of spring, planting is a major activity
accompanied by historical accounts that may interest children.
The illustrations range from diagrams to cartoons and are
equally appealing to children and adults. *Blood and Guts*, which
follows a similar format, has to do with understanding the body
and its functions. These books offer to teachers many
possibilities to integrate science in the curriculum creatively
and to parents an opportunity to develop activities with their
children that will be of interest to both of them.

Allison, Linda. *Summer Book/The Wild Inside.* Boston, Mass.:
    Sierra Club Books/Little, Brown & Co., 1979.

Both books have a unique style that makes the obvious very
special. Everyday materials and environments are used to
create phenomena through activities and children's scientific
investigations.
Summer Book is divided into 14 parts and includes such
topics as Sun Power, Keep Cool, Conservation, Sleeping Out,
and Trips. Well-designed diagrams and drawings complement
the write-up of the activities.
The Wild Inside uses a similar technique. It is a great
resource for children who have to spend time indoors, since the
activities aim to simulate as much as possible of the outdoors,
indoors.
It is divided in four parts, with intriguing headings: Taking
Shelter, Wild and Not So Wild, Mountains in the House, and

House Happenings. Both books are great resources for families, after-school programs, camps, and nature centers.

Althouse, Rosemary. *Investigating Science with Young Children.* New York: Teachers College Press, 1988.

The author emphasizes that the process approach is the most effective for young children to experience science. The activities are drawn from her real-life situations, as well as from those of other preschool teachers who have engaged three- to five-year-olds in scientific investigations successfully.

The book is divided into two parts: Part I sets up the theoretical framework of what the process approach is and how it can be adapted to children's developmental stages.

Part II includes 85 activities that are based on the children's immediate environments, water, color, pets, seeds, foods, bubbles, and working with wood.

The write-up of each activity is very explicit and inviting for teachers and children. The integrity of the scientific method is carried throughout the book.

Althouse, Rosemary, and Cecil Main, Jr. *Science Experiences for Young Children.* New York: Teachers College Press, 1975.

A series of booklets thematically organized with topics related to children's daily experiences (As We Grow, Colors, Food, Magnets, Pets, Seeds, and Wheels). Each booklet includes a rationale for the topic in its brief introduction. The activities are explicit and state the concept, questions to be answered through investigation, materials, procedures, and comments on developmental issues as they relate to each activity. The illustrations are indicative of the informality that characterizes this book. A brief but well-chosen bibliography concludes each booklet. Packaged in a bright cardboard casing, they are easy to store in the classroom. A practical resource for teachers of young children.

Amery, Heather. *The Know How Book of Experiments.* Tulsa,
Okla: EDC, 1977.

This book is written for teachers of younger and older
children and focuses on air, water, optics, and plants. It
presents the process and content of a series of experiments in
science in a combination of pictures, sketches, diagrams, and
text. The materials are from the child's environment and can be
used as an enrichment to a hands-on science curriculum for
schoolchildren, as well as for after-school programs.

Ardley, Neil. *Air.* / *Color.* / *Light.* / *Water.* San Diego, Calif.:
Harcourt Brace Jovanovich, 1991.

This series of attractive, colorful books uses clearly stated
pictorial representations of science-based activities. The text
presents the elements of inquiry, and a concluding paragraph
connects the findings to the real world around us.

All four books are a valuable resource for the teacher who is
reluctant to engage in science. The attractive, realistic
illustrations are an invitation for hands-on scientific
explorations.

Arnold, Lois B. *Preparing Young Children for Science: A Book of
Activities.* New York: Schocken Books, 1980.

The activities are based on the COPES science curriculum
and adapted to young (five to eight years old) children's levels
of development and interest. The science concepts refer to
properties of things, measuring, ecology and environments,
patterns, and relationships. The content is taken from
children's environments. For example, the chapter "Properties
of Things" includes investigations of properties such as color,
shape, texture, magnetism, and germination, using the
appropriate materials. The author encourages parents and
teachers to explore with children the science concepts that
apply to materials and phenomena. A list of related science

books for adults and young children further enhance the use of this book.

Benesch, Jane, and Beth Bergman. *Science Discovery—An Approach to Preschool Science Education.* Baltimore, Md.: Maryland Science Center, 1988.

This book is the result of science education programs developed for four- to five-year-olds by the Maryland Science Center.

The authors' approach to teaching science is developmentally appropriate, and is based on content that interests preschoolers, such as Animal Habitats, Natural Environments, Bodily Functions, and Simple Machines. The strategies are activity-based and incorporate inquiry skills, as well as simulations and dramatic play. The extended activities relate to the children's lives and incorporate literature, music, and art.

This book invites teachers to involve young children in science explorations.

Blackwelder, Sheila Keyser. *Science for All Seasons.* Englewood Cliffs, N.J.: Prentice Hall, 1980.

The author recommends that the scientific process be used as a way to explore the content of the book and encourages teachers to engage children in open discussions so they may further clarify their investigations and findings. The seasonal approach facilitates the scheduling of science in the school calendar and relates it to curriculum. The content of the book is organized into: Fall (the physical self, anatomy), Winter (frost and snow, electricity, magnets, light and shadows, crystals, rocks, volcanos, dinosaurs and birds), Spring (weather, spring as a season, environment, pollution), and Summer (insects, fish, shells, stars). The author supplements each activity with introductory notes to the teacher and extensive readings and bibliography. Each topic combines content with process skills and suggestions to teachers on how to guide children to "get results" and "find out phenomena."

Booth, Gerry. *The Big Beast Book.* Boston, Mass.: Little, Brown & Co./Yolla Bolly Press, 1988.

The book is part of a series of activity books written for children and adults by a group of California teachers, writers, and artists based on their classroom experiences. It addresses the theme of dinosaurs, which is of great interest to children.

It combines science concepts on fossils with activities that motivate children to go beyond the "magic" of dinosaurs. It presents opportunities for both younger and older children to get involved in investigations of dinosaurs.

Teachers as well as parents can benefit from this creative approach that includes a wide range of possibilities for children to investigate inside as well as outside the classroom. A great sourcebook for dinosaurmaniacs!

Bourgeois, Paulette. *The Amazing Dirt Book.* Reading, Mass.: Addison-Wesley Publishing Co., 1990.

This unorthodox book includes all the possible functions of "dirt"—from the burial of antiquities to footprints to our own personal encounters, as well as life to be found in dirt. In addition, it provides historical information on how people cleaned their own dirt in the past and other interesting topics.

Activities include investigating footprints and making casts of them, constructing sand sculpture, investigating types of dirt (composts and gardening), and exploring city dumps. Titles of chapters are (1) You and Dirt, (2) Buried, (3) The "Dirt" on Dirt, (4) Dirt Homes, and (5) Dirt for Gardening.

The text is illustrated with drawings. The combination is inviting for "dirt" explorations.

Bowder, Marcia. *Nature for the Very Young.* New York: John Wiley & Sons, 1989.

This book, written for teachers of preschool children, is divided in four parts: Autumn, Winter, Spring, and Summer. The content is a combination of information on habitats and nature in general that is intended for teachers and hands-on activities for children.

The activities are focused on outdoor and indoor nature study. The author provides guidelines on how to integrate the science of nature with language, art, music, and body movement and how to adapt the lessons to children's developmental levels.

The book is more valuable as a reference to nature study than as a curriculum in itself.

Bowman, Mary Lynne, and Herbert L. Cook. *Recycling Activities for the Classroom*. Columbus, Ohio: ERIC/SMEAC, Ohio State University, 1978.

This book addresses the environmental issues of recycling as an alternative to increasing the use of natural resources and to reduce solid wastes. The authors have developed activities for students in all grades and classified them accordingly. The format of presentation for each activity includes purpose, grade level, subject matter (science, math, social studies, language arts), references, and the activity itself, which incorporates questions to be answered by the students through their investigations. The authors promote teacher initiative and encourage children's decision-making in their involvement and their findings. The thematic emphasis of this book and the valuable appendixes of resources make it particularly important and valuable as a tool for environmental education.

Brown, Sam, ed. *Bubbles, Rainbows and Worms—Science Experiments for Preschool Children*. Mt. Rainier, Md.: Gryphon House, 1981.

The author bases the activities of the book on the assumption that children develop science concepts through the knowledge they gain as they investigate the properties of the physical world. In the ten commandments for teaching science to young children, the author emphasizes the need for children to be in charge of the investigations and findings and for teachers to facilitate the process. This popularized recipe-like activities book is easy to follow, includes helpful illustrations, and uses materials that interest children and are easy to obtain. The content is organized along the lines of such familiar topics as animals, plants, environment, senses, and water, and includes a series of miscellaneous activities involving magnets, food, and wheels. A suggested list of children's books follows each chapter.

Butzow, Carol M., and John W. Butzow. *Science through Children's Literature. An Integrated Approach.* Englewood, Colo.: Teacher Ideas Press, 1989.

The authors acknowledge that both reading and science are processes that must involve the learner actively. The book addresses grades K–3 and supports the integrated approach to learning. (Long overdue!)

The content is divided in four parts: (1) Using Children's Literature as a Springboard to Science, (2) Life Science, (3) Earth and Space Science, and (4) Physical Science.

Although the concepts related to integrating science to reading are on target, the selection of children's books that are analyzed narrows the choices from the wide range of available collections. The discussion and illustration of concept mapping for relating science to literature is useful, and an experienced teacher will be able to adjust it to different developmental levels.

The bibliography on children's books reflects the author's choices.

Candler, Laura. *Science Club Companion.* Riverview, Fla.: Idea Factory, 1989.

This is an effort to bring science into the lives of children as an extracurricular learning experience. It is a valuable reference for teachers/parents and organizations that want to expand their role to nonformal science education.

Chapter One offers a wide range of ideas and suggestions on how to organize a science club; Chapter Two presents ideas on topics to be included and on how to organize activities; and Chapter Three gives a wide range of resources, from NSTA to supplies of science-based materials.

These guidelines respond to current interests in science for children from kindergarten to the upper elementary grades.

Carmichael, Viola S. *Science Experiences for Young Children.* 4th Printing. Sierra Madre, Calif.: S. California Association for the Education of Young Children (P.O. Box 691), 1973.

This typed manual on science experiences is direct and informal in its approach. It emphasizes the scientific method as a way of finding out and requires that children get involved with materials. It integrates art and language throughout the science investigations and offers tips on raising children's interest levels. The topics include rocks, soil fossils, plants and animals, weather, outer space, day and night, airplanes and rockets, the human body, senses, cooking, machines, electricity, and magnets. Each unit includes science information for teachers, strategies for teaching, and ideas for class projects that include the arts. A valuable reference for teachers who want to integrate science investigations in the curriculum.

Carson, Mary Stetten. *The Scientific Kid.* New York: Harper and Row, 1989.

This informal, handwritten book treats each science exploration as a children's discovery.

It is a hands-on collection of 35 experiments, each of which is a two-page display. The first page is pictorial and depicts the child or children in action, while the second page gives step-by-step directions in a cartoonlike sequence with drawings and subtitles on how to proceed with the experiment.

It can be a fun book for parents, too. The materials are inexpensive and from our everyday environment. The author encourages grown-ups to stand back and allow children to express their thoughts and feelings about what is happening.

The topics include growing crystal; exploring the senses; and making things, such as pinhole cameras, a mini movie, and a periscope, as well as many activities involving the outdoors—kites, bird feeders, bubbles, parachutes, and sprouting seeds.

Claycomb, Patty. *Love the Earth.* Livonia, Miss.: Partner Press, 1991.

Attitudes develop early in life, and this book aims to do just that for young children. "Love the Earth" is the main purpose of this book, and it is presented through an integrated approach to learning for young children. The titles of the chapters—Earth Discoveries, Sharing the Earth, Colors of the Earth, Earth Songs, and Fingerplays—describe the author's intent.

The activities take place indoors and outdoors and encourage children to explore, discover, and communicate their thoughts and feelings. Helpful suggestions enhance the use of this book, which is a valuable resource in an early childhood learning environment.

Cobb, Vicki. *Science Experiments You Can Eat.* New York: J.B. Lippincott, 1974.

The author focuses on various aspects of cooking and eating as means of teaching science. For example, she identifies scientific processes such as experimentation and science concepts such as change and uses the activity of beating egg whites to stiff peaks to teach them to children. The book is a good resource to supplement any science programs that include nutrition or the exploration of chemistry concepts in everyday living.

Cohen, Michael R., and Larry Flick, Eds. *Expanding Children's Thinking through Science, CESI Sourcebook II.* Columbus, Ohio: ERIC/SMEAC, 1981.

This sourcebook challenges teachers' rational thinking, as well as creativity. Although the materials used are from our everyday environment, the activities tend to be challenging and problem oriented to stimulate children's curiosity and thinking, especially older children in the elementary grades.

They are organized under such topics as creativity, problem solving, values, self-esteem, visual thinking, and inventions.

Most of the challenges and problems address older children's thinking in the elementary grades.

Science is treated as part of life, as a way of thinking about issues that concern our daily existence, not as an isolated activity in a laboratory situation.

The book is useful for individuals who want to look in depth at issues in science education.

Coon, Herbert L., and Michele Y. Alexander. *Energy Activities for the Classroom.* Columbus, Ohio: Ohio State University Press, 1976.

The rationale for these selected energy teaching activities is based on the urgency of energy problems that have emerged in our world. The authors urge teachers to involve students in understanding the science of energy and in exploring the diversity of solutions on energy issues. Each teaching activity states purpose, grade level (K–12), subject matter (basically science, but other subjects may be included), concept, and the activity itself. The authors emphasize the scientific process as a way of exploring and arriving at solutions to the existing problems. A well-documented and organized resource for teachers.

Cornell, Joseph B. *Sharing Nature with Children.* Nevada City, Calif.: Amanda Publications, 1979.

This modest paperback includes valuable tips and activities for adults on how to organize nature walks with children, what experiences to provide, and how to enhance, share, and enjoy children's discoveries in the natural world. The author understands how children learn effectively and what interests them. He encourages sensory explorations like observing smells and sounds and microhiking on your belly with a magnifying glass. He utilizes games and simulations to explain life cycles and animal behaviors. He encourages aesthetic appreciation along with scientific exploration and enthusiastically urges parents and teachers to share nature with children.

Couchman, T.K., Y.C. MacBean, A. Stecher, and D.F. Wentworth. *Examining Your Environment.* 12 vols. Minneapolis, Minn.: Winston Press, 1976.

A series of 12 paperback books written for teachers who want to teach environmental science in a creative and effective way. Each book is organized thematically and does not require great knowledge on the topic by the teacher. Each activity starts with a question to be investigated and can be used independently or in a sequence. Children's interest and age level is considered all through the books. A bibliography and glossary is found at the end of each book. All activities are field tested and the books are illustrated with natural wonders, children's work, diagrams, and documentation on children's findings. The very attractive and dynamic texts will motivate even the most hesitant teacher to get involved in environmental investigations. *Examining Your Environment* titles: (1) Astronomy, (2) Birds, (3) Dandelion, (4) Ecology, (5) Mapping Small Plans, (6) Mini-Climates, (7) Running Water, (8) Small Creatures, (9) Snow and Ice, (10) Trees, and (11) Your Senses.

DeVito, Alfred, and Gerald H. Krockover. *Creative Sciencing Ideas and Activities for Teachers and Children.* 2nd ed. Boston, Mass.: Little, Brown, 1960.

This book is a natural companion to the author's book *Creative Sciencing—A Practical Approach.* It is a resource book organized by activities that emphasize a combination of subject matter and science skills. The format used to cross-reference the science skills with the content must be well understood before the book is utilized in science teaching. An understanding of children's developmental stages is also a prerequisite for teachers so they may adapt the activities appropriately. The activities are independent of each other, the style of presentation is original, and many projects incorporate other subjects so that children may better understand the role of science in their lives and not treat it as a separate entity. Teachers are encouraged to do their own brainstorming on how to use the activities more effectively and ideas are offered on how to motivate the students to get involved.

Section I includes 130 activities and cross-references them between science skills and subject matter. Section II provides suggestions on how to develop resources on a minimum budget. Section III focuses on techniques such as soldering, setting up circuits, and so forth. Section IV offers 20 creative recipes that incorporate science concepts but can be used in other subjects of the curriculum: pastes, dyes, printing ink, bubble solutions, and so forth. Appendix A cross-references science activities with other subjects. Conversion tables and bibliographies follow.

Elementary Science Study. 33 vols. New York: McGraw-Hill, 1969.

These activity-centered books represent joint efforts of scientists and teachers from many disciplines with a unified view on how children may learn science more effectively and enjoyably. Their purpose is to help a teacher make the classroom a laboratory where children can adapt their learning to their developmental stages and levels of interest. Content and scientific process are combined in a flexible scheme where children control their investigations and record their findings, while the teacher facilitates and guides the science study. Each book can be used independently as well as a resource to further explore a topic of science. The activity-centered books are listed below according to the area of science study, title of unit, and grade level:

Physical Science: Light and Shadow (K–3), Mobiles (K–4), Spinning Tables (1–2), Mirror Cards (1–6), Sink and Float (2–7), Clay Boats (2–8), Drop Streams and Containers (3–4), Mystery Powders (3–4), Ice Cubes (3–5), and Colored Solutions (3–8).

Biological Sciences: Growing Seeds (K–3), Life of Beans and Peas (K–4), Butterflies (K–5), Eggs and Tadpoles (K–6), Animals in Classroom (K–9), Brine Shrimp (1–4), Changes (1–4), Pond Water (1–7), Starting from Seeds (3–7), and Mosquitoes (3–9).

Earth Sciences: Daytime Astronomy (1–8), Sand (2–3), Rocks and Charts (3–6), Where Is the Moon? (3–7).

General Skills: Match and Measure (K–3), Primary Balancing (K–4), Pattern Blocks (K–6), Geo Blocks (K–6), A tangram (K–8), Musical Instrument Recipe Book (K–9), Attribute Games and Problems (K–9), Printing (1–6), and Structures (2–6).

Forte, Imogene, and Joy MacKenzie. *Creative Science Experiences for the Young Child.* Nashville, Tenn.: Incentive Publications, 1983.

The authors intend to give children concrete experiences of the physical world around them. The book is divided into five chapters: Living Things; The Human Body; Earth and Sky; Air and Water; and Machines, Magnets, and Electricity.

The organization and presentation of the book follow the traditional textbook design. Every page can be torn out, duplicated, and given to the students to complete. Suggested activities require the teacher's input and uniform involvement by the students. There is an abundance of scientific information and explanations to be delivered by the teachers.

This book will be helpful to teachers in traditional classrooms who want to control the hands-on science experimentation.

Forte, Imogene, and Sandra Schurr. *Exploring Science.* Nashville, Tenn.: Incentive Publications, 1988.

This book combines several aspects of the teaching of science.

It selects topics from earth, life, and physical science. The activities around each topic adhere to the hierarchy of Bloom's taxonomy; for example, on rocks, the activities are sequenced to reflect knowledge, comprehension, application, analysis, synthesis, and evaluation.

The lower levels of the hierarchy are applicable to younger children, while the higher levels address older children's thinking capabilities.

The activities are divided between hands-on and the book/worksheet type. The challenges and explorations are part of everyday life and involve children in very structured ways.

Gardner, Robert, and David Webster. *Science in Your Backyard.* Englewood Cliffs, N.J.: Julian Messner, 1987.

One more resource book for teachers (and parents) on how children can investigate their immediate physical environments.

It is a descriptive book on how to follow nature's clues for living organisms, how to begin collections, how to observe phenomena, and how to construct experiments to find out.

Most of the investigations are focused on older children in the elementary grades; however, the ideas have a universal appeal and can be adapted for children in the primary grades.

A supportive reference to an environmental science curriculum.

An appendix of scientific supply companies is helpful for teachers and parents.

George, K.D., M.A. Dietz, and E.C. Abraham. *Science Investigations for Elementary School Teachers.* Boston, Mass.: D.C. Heath, 1974.

A supplement to the book by K.D. George et al. The investigations are structured according to specific objective materials to be used and procedures to be followed. The appendixes further clarify for teachers the science concepts and children's learning outcomes. Although the content will interest children of all ages, this book will be most appropriate for children at the higher grades.

Goldstein-Jackson, Kevin. *Experiments with Everyday Objects: Science Activities for Children, Parents and Teachers.* Englewood Cliffs, N.J.: Prentice Hall, 1978.

The author seeks to increase the level of interest in science for children and adults through a series of experiments. The materials used are familiar and each experiment reflects its own science concept and subject matter. The content is organized into seven categories: air and water pressure, buoyancy, surface tension, mechanics, chemistry, color and candles, viewing and drawing, and electricity and magnetism. Each experiment is illustrated for further clarification and can be used independently of the others. The variety of experiments is wide and they border on the element of magic (if you don't know the scientific explanations that go with them). There is an expected result for each experiment and the author assumes that understanding will emerge from performance. A resource for the teacher or parent who knows science and is looking for experiments to do together with children.

Graf, Rudolf F. *Safe and Simple Electrical Experiments.* New York: Dover Publications, 1973.

A heavily illustrated book on electrical experiments that is easy to follow for teachers, parents, and children. There are 38 experiments in static electricity, 31 on magnets, and 31 on current electricity and electromagnetism. The materials used are simple, safe, and easy to find, and the activities are for children in K–6 grades. Two pages on the history of discoveries in electricity offer an extra point of interest for older children. A valuable sourcebook for classrooms that engage in the teaching of electricity and magnetism.

GREAT EXPLORATIONS IN MATH AND SCIENCE (GEMS) *Animal Defenses/ Buzzing a Hive/ Hide a Butterfly/ Liquid Exploration/ Involving Dissolving/ Wizard's Lab.* Berkeley, Calif.: Lawrence Hall of Science, University of California at Berkeley, 1988.

These six GEMS booklets are part of a wider collection of teachers' guides on science.

They are designed for grades K–3 and give detailed instructions to teachers on how to engage children in scientific explorations using inquiry skills. At the same time, they encourage flexibility and can be adapted to different teaching situations. In general, they promote independence, creativity, and critical thinking. Mathematical concepts are applied whenever needed and in ways that make sense to children.

The first three books are based on life sciences and the themes are developmentally appropriate and easily integrated in the curriculum. The remaining three books are based on physical science and engage children in hands-on investigations.

The series is reminiscent of the Elementary Science Study series of the 1960s.

Green, Bea, and Sandi Schlichting. *Explorations and Investigations.* Riverview, Fla.: Idea Factory, 1985.

This informal collection of science hands-on explorations, packaged in a three-ring binder, gives step-by-step directions to teachers so they can overcome their apprehension about teaching science to young children. It also lists appropriate questions and presents detailed descriptions of how to engage in scientific investigations, collect data, and make graphs.

Reproducible teacher-directed charts and record-keeping sheets are available. The following are examples of teacher-directed scientific investigations: sinking and floating objects in water, finding seeds in fruits, planting seeds, making popcorn, magnets, melting ice, and so forth.

Griffin, Margaret, and Deborah Seed. *The Amazing Egg Book.* Reading, Mass.: Addison-Wesley Publishing Co. 1989.

A versatile sourcebook on studying farm animals, birds, and nutrition, among other things. It could also be described as "all you ever wanted to know about eggs"—from myths to cooking, from art to the kinds of eggs, hatching a chick, egg explorations, and how animals protect their eggs. A resource companion for teachers and parents who practice an integrated approach to teaching and learning. The "let us find out" approach qualifies this book for the science activities category.

Habben, Dorothy. *Science Experiments That Really Work.* Chicago: Follett Publishing Co., 1970.

According to the author, this activity book includes field tested experiments that have motivated children to investigate and answer questions on their own. The activities are organized into seven parts and include experiments with air, carbon dioxide, heat, crystals, magnets, electricity, and sound. Several activities are described in each category, and each experiment ends with a key question for the child to answer. The illustrated activities can be used independently or as a supplement in other physical science curricula. The materials are simple and easy to find. A special section—"more about each experiment"—can assist children to explore further science concepts.

Haldary, D.F., and S.H. Cohen. *Laboratory Science and Art for Blind, Deaf and Emotionally Disturbed Children: A Mainstreaming Approach.* Baltimore, Md.: University Park Press, 1978.

This comprehensive book is based on years of experience in the adaptation of science curricula (SCIS, SAPA and ESS) to the teaching of blind, deaf, and emotionally disturbed children. Appropriate counterpart art activities are proposed that will further enhance the children's development of science concepts. The book is organized into four sections. Section I offers both a convincing rationale why science and art are important in the educational process of handicapped children and information on how to integrate and mainstream them. A helpful chart cross references the science with the art activities. Section II classifies and develops the science activities. Each activity includes exploration by the child, the science concept it teaches, materials and procedures, and adaptation for each handicap. A brief Section III presents useful background on science and material for teachers, and Section IV describes art activities in a way similar to science activities (Section II). This is a most valuable book for preservice and inservice teachers and administrators in elementary education. The 50 science and 63 art lessons are supportive evidence for effective mainstreaming. The illustrators depict children's involvement and strengthen further the authors' views on science and art study for the handicapped.

Hapai, Marlene Nachbar, and Leon H. Burton. *Bug Play Activities with Insects for Young Children* (plus a cassette with bug sounds). Reading, Mass.: Addison-Wesley Publishing Co., 1990.

The book combines a wide range of knowledge about insects, as well as strategies on how to engage children in studying and appreciating insects.

This valuable resource is divided in three sections.

Part 1, Introduction, presents valuable information on how to utilize the book: how to handle insects and adapt the lessons to different age groups.

Part 2, The Lessons, is organized as individual lessons on the 26 insects. Each lesson includes a knowledge base about the insecT—anatomy, habitats, life-style—as well as strategies on how to engage children inside and outside the classroom.

A special feature is the songs and music written for each insect. The cassette offers real-life sounds of the insects, too.

The book is very attractive, interspersed with pictures of children's investigations and accurate diagrams of insects.

Herbert, Don. *Mr. Wizard's Supermarket Science.* New York: Random House, 1980.

The book is based on Mr. Wizard's television show and focuses on the products of supermarkets and the science activities that can be generated from them. The author claims that "functional fixedness" of objects prevents students from using them creatively. Thus, he uses products of a supermarket to explore science concepts. For example, milk-based glue, vinegar rocket launches, gelatin stalagmites, cereal box cameras, and so forth. There is an element of sensationalism in the book, but in the hands of a teacher with science knowledge it can provide creative science explorations for children. Each activity is independent and can supplement any science program.

Herbert, Don, and H. Ruchlis. *Mr. Wizard's 400 Experiments in Science.* Brooklyn, N.Y.: Book-Lab, 1968.

A series of science experiments with diagrams and detailed directions using materials that are easily found in our immediate surroundings. This book will be useful to a teacher who is knowledgeable about science and wants more experiments and projects to enrich science teachings.

Herman, Marina L., Joseph F. Passineau, Ann L. Schimpf, and Paul Treuer. *Teaching Kids to Love the Earth.* Duluth, Minn.: Pfeifer-Hamilton Publishers, 1991.

This book invites the teacher and learner to get involved in an adventure through science. The topic is the Earth, and the 185 activities are based on a commitment to and enjoyment in finding out about the physical aspects of this planet and their implications for living things, as the chapter titles—Curiosity, Exploration, Discovery, Sharing, Passion, A Final Invitation—indicate.

Every page is full of surprises—most of which appeal to our common sense.

Teaching and learning are interwoven. Young children can become part of the adventure as long as adults keep their curiosity, explorations, and discoveries on course (developmentally appropriate).

Parents as well as teachers can use this book, which combines hands-on, reading, reflecting, and feeling activities.

Hill, Katherine E. *Exploring the Natural World with Young Children.* New York: Harcourt Brace Jovanovich, 1976.

The author believes that children's exploration of natural phenomena is as important to their development as other aspects of their preschool experiences. The suggested experiences in science are grouped into themes such as air, water, cooking, inside things, light, sound, moving things, our earth, space, animals, and plants. Each topic includes concepts to be formulated, materials to be used, procedures to follow, questions for the teacher to ask and possible children's answers, and appropriate age levels. The materials are simple, the style informal and direct, and, although there are no illustrations, the book is easy to follow.

Hoffman, Helen Marie, and H. and Kenneth S. Ricker. *Sourcebook in Science Education and the Physically Handicapped.* Washington, D.C., NSTA, 1979.

This publication is the result of a working conference sponsored by the National Science Teachers Association in 1977. It is a valuable sourcebook for teachers who have physically handicapped students in their science classes. The topics discussed are: science education for the handicapped; science for the auditorily, orthopedically, and visually handicapped; and science programs beyond the school.

Possible careers in science and related fields are discussed, as well as the future implications of science education for the physically handicapped. The sections on the science for the auditorily, orthopedically, and visually handicapped offer valuable background and activities for the teacher. The extensive bibliographies complement each section effectively. The input of so many scholars in this field contributes immensely to the usefulness of this publication.

Hone, Elizabeth B., Alexander Joseph, and Edward Victor. *A Sourcebook for Elementary Science.* 2nd ed. New York: Harcourt Brace Jovanovich, 1971.

A traditional, comprehensive sourcebook on science and classroom activities written for elementary school teachers. The detailed diagrams and photographs contribute greatly to an understanding of how the extensive science content of the activities works. The book is organized thematically along biological, physical, and earth science lines and it includes topics of technology such as machines and engines, communications, radioactivity, fibers and clothing, space travel, and flight. Although the scope of the book focuses on science for older children, many of the activities can be adapted for very young children. An extensive bibliography follows each chapter.

Jacobson, Willard, and Abby Bergman. *Science Activities for Children.* Englewood Cliffs, N.J.: Prentice Hall, 1983.

This book of science activities is for adults who plan science experiences for children at home, in school, or at camp. The content is organized thematically: plants and animals, air, water and weather, energy (heat, light, and solar), studying ourselves, the earth, magnetism and electricity, and making and exploring the universe. A brief introduction that includes rationale and instruction precedes the activities of each specific theme. Each activity is independent and is organized with title, age group, type of investigation, materials, procedures, and a section on enrichment. The materials are simple and inexpensive, and the authors emphasize the importance of enjoyment and involvement as key components of children's science experiences. A valuable resource for homes and camps and for existing science curriculum in the elementary classroom.

Jaffe, Roberta, and Gary Appel. *The Growing Classroom— Garden-Based Science*. Reading, Mass.: Addison-Wesley Publishing Co., 1990.

A comprehensive sourcebook for teachers who teach about the environment, specifically, those who engage children in learning about the relationship of plant life and nutrition, life cycles, climates, and garden ecology.

The book is divided in three sections plus an appendix.

Section I, "Breaking Ground," gives valuable information on how to start a school garden, inside and outside the classroom. Section II includes the science of the curriculum—indoor-outdoor activities on ecology, life cycles, climates, and so forth. Section III engages children in nutritional science—foods, nutrients, and appropriate consumer behavior.

The format for each activity is easy to implement, and the age appropriateness of each activity is given. Tips on managing the activity and time lines for completing it are valuable for the teacher. The use of science process skills in the hands-on investigations is described. Furthermore, math, language, art, music, and social skills are integrated and cooperative learning is encouraged.

The appendix provides a wide range of useful information on equipment, planting guides, scope and sequential charts, a complete materials list for each unit, an English-Spanish vocabulary list, a list of seed companies, and other resources.

Johns, Frank D., Kurt Allen Liske, and Amy L. Evans. *Education Goes Outdoors*. Reading, Mass.: Addison-Wesley Publishing Co., 1986.

This truly integrated outdoor curriculum for developing environmental awareness is a valuable sourcebook. It presents ideas on how to use materials, resources, and strategies for enhancing the school curriculum with outdoor learning experiences.

It qualifies as a science sourcebook because of the scientific process skills used as teaching strategies. The real-life situations provide a motivational base for the children. The chapters include Sensitivity to the Environment, Outdoor Language Activities, Schoolyard Math Investigations, Art Experiences in Nature, Explorations in Social Studies, Science Beyond the Classroom, and Discovering the Community.

It is recommended for afterschool programs, camps, and parents, as well as for teachers.

Although it can be adapted for younger children (4–6 years), it is most appropriate for 7 to 10 year olds.

Jones-Hoyt, Nancy, and Scott Shane. *One Thing Leads to Another—Ideas for Creative Discovery with Children.* Boston, Mass.: Wheelock College, 1988.

This publication is one of the many ways Wheelock College celebrated its centennial (1888–1988). Early childhood education has been Wheelock's mission for 100 years, and the college is going strong.

This loose-leaf publication documents 51 activities that provide ideas for creative learning for young children.

The hands-on emphasis offers opportunities for children to construct their own knowledge of the world around them.

Each activity is followed by a content pathway that the authors documented as they brainstormed about the theme.

Taking a cue from the title *One Thing Leads to Another,* the authors encourage parents and early childhood professionals to take their own pathways and adapt them to their own children and environments. A fun, creative resource for young children's explorations.

Jurek, Dianne, and Sharon MacDonald. *Discovering the World—Physical Science*. Allen, Tex.: DLM Teaching Resources, 1989.

A hands-on physical science activity book for teachers of young children that is divided into three parts. Part One is brief, with concrete ideas on how to set up and manage a discovery center in the classroom. Part Two contains 40 activities that are based on physical science and on the immediate physical environment of the children, e.g., water, cooking, kites, shadow play, simple machines, ramps, and cars. Part Three is a series of working papers that correspond to the activities and can be torn out, reproduced, and offered as pictorial guides to the children. The language part is appropriate for children in the early primary grades. The activities are clearly presented and helpful for a hands-on, teacher-directed science class, especially for the teacher who is not sure how to involve children in learning about science.

Kaner, Etta. *Balloon Science*. Reading, Mass.: Addison-Wesley Publishing Co., 1989.

Balloon science is what it claims to be. The attractive package of colorful balloons attached to the cover invites the reader to engage immediately in balloon-air explorations.

The collection of activities, interspersed with black-and-white cartoonlike displays on how to use balloons and how to motivate children to investigate the balloons. The scientific process skills are enhanced by questions that appear all through the book.

Parents, teachers, and friends of children will enjoy sharing this book with children.

An instantly welcome gift!

Katz, Adrienne. *Naturewatch—Exploring Nature with Children*. Reading, Mass.: Addison-Wesley Publishing Co., 1986.

This book encourages adults and children to engage in projects that are based on the wonders of nature. It is not a "how-to" book, but is inviting, aesthetically pleasing, and full of ideas about how to get involved in finding out and appreciating at the same time. Poetry and accurate drawings support the author's goals.

The projects can be done in any sequence and are designed to raise children's curiosity and aesthetic appreciation of nature.

The book is divided into the following sections: Growing Aware, A Closer Look at Plants, A Garden of Your Own, Garden Visitors, Birds, Trees, Finds, Plant Crafts, Plant Magic, and Useful Lists.

An activity-filled reference book for teachers, parents, camp leaders, and afterschool programs.

Knight, Michael E., and Terry L. Graham. *The Leaves Are Falling in Rainbows*. Atlanta, Ga.: Humanics, 1984.

A sourcebook of science activities related to young children's daily experiences. The teacher facilitates hands-on investigations for the children. The activities are organized thematically in nine chapters: Water, Air, Plants and Growth, Light, Shadows, Magnets, Sound, Changes, and Electricity.

A rationale introduces each chapter and is followed by a list of easily available materials, as well as the key concepts to be investigated.

Each activity is introduced with a question that leads children to explorations. Easy-to-follow charts help teachers document children's findings.

The book enriches the early childhood curriculum and helps teachers to engage young children in doing science.

Levenson, Elaine. *Teaching Children About Science*. New York: Prentice Hall, 1985.

The author encourages adults to engage children in hands-on science.

The activities provide science information, appropriate questions, resources, and diagrams that facilitate the organization of the activity. The book is divided in ten chapters. The Introduction proposes teaching strategies and developmental appropriateness and urges adults to support children's investigations and findings. The next chapter presents models of instruction to be implemented in the following eight chapters. The topics under investigation are the five senses, magnetism, static electricity, sound, light, air, water, weather, volcanoes, rock, and erosion.

The science and the teaching strategies suggested are applicable to children in the second to fourth grade.

Lewis, James. *Learn While You Scrub Science in the Tub.* Deephaven, Minn.: Meadowbrook Press, 1989.

A sequel to the previous book. The activities encourage hands-on involvement for children five years old and above. The science content—Why did it happen?—addresses the adult's need to "know," while the actual explorations contribute to the children's understanding of how water behaves.

Both books belong in the classroom, as well as in the children's homes.

Lewis, James. *Rub-a-Dub-Dub Science in the Tub.* Deephaven, Minn.: Meadowbrook Press, 1989.

The activities are based on water inside and outside the bathtub. The book is directed to parents, but can be applied in preschool environments where water is made available for children (two to five years) to explore.

The illustrations and brief text help adults get children involved. The science content is more appropriate for adults, but the hands-on explorations are definitely appropriate for children.

Lingelbach, Genepher (Ed.). *Hands on Nature.* Woodstock, VT: Vermont Institute of Natural Science, 1986.

This book is a tribute to environmental education.

The knowledge base on the environment of the Northern Hemisphere is immense. Furthermore, the organization of the content and the conceptual framework are creative and exciting for learners, whether they are adults or children.

The chapter titles are Adaptation, Habitats, Cycles, and Designs of Nature. Animal and plant life are interwoven in the content. The teaching strategies originated in workshops and rely heavily on hands-on scientific investigations. The sequence and materials follow the seasonal cycle of the Northern Hemisphere.

The activities are independent of each other, can be adapted to any age group, and will enhance any environmental science curriculum.

Extensions to the science-based investigations include puppetry, language arts, art projects, math, and affective objectives.

The overall goal of this monumental work is to foster a positive attitude toward the environment.

The exhaustive reading lists for children are coded for age appropriateness.

The drawings are life-like and contribute to the effectiveness of the activities.

An essential resource for any school, camp, or after-school program.

Macdonald Educational Science 5/13. Set I. Milwaukee, Wis.: Macdonald-Raintree, 1974.

A team effort of British educators, including members of the Nuffield Foundation, has produced a series of books with science topics that children are most likely to want to investigate. They are books for adults who teach children between the ages of five and 13. Each book is organized thematically, taking into consideration children's developmental stages, the integration of science in the curriculum, children's interests, investigations, findings, and recordings.

They are field tested and well-documented, with photographs, diagrams, and children's readings.

Each book has a chief author and a working team, and can be used independently of the other books in the set. These dynamic, child-centered science teaching books can be helpful to teachers who share the author's views on how children can learn science more effectively.

Science 5/13 titles: (1) Working with Wood, (2) Time, (3) Early Experiences, (4) Structures and Forces, in two volumes, (5) Science from Toys, (6) Minibeasts, (7) Holes, Gaps and Cavities, (8) Metals, (9) Change, in two volumes, (10) Trees, (11) Like and Unlike, in two volumes, (12) Coloured Things, and (13) Children and Plastic. *Using the Environment*: (1) Early Experiences, (2) Investigations, (3) Tackling Problems, and (4) Ways and Means.

Markle, Sandra. *Exploring Spring.* New York: Macmillan Publishing Co., 1990.

A comprehensive view of spring—about the rebirth of plants, animals, and all the phenomena that come with the season.

The style is a narrative on the happenings and on how to engage children in an investigation and appreciation of their findings. The drawings are in black and white and contribute to the overall effectiveness of the text. Riddles and games are interspersed, too.

A sourcebook for teachers with many instructional tips on how to motivate children to explore and enjoy the season. The author's other books on seasons are *Exploring Winter* and *Exploring Summer.*

McGavack, John, Jr., and Donald P. LaSalle. *Guppies, Bubbles and Vibrating Objects.* New York: The John Day Co., 1969.

This book offers strategies and science activities to help children have experiences very similar to those of scientists. The authors begin with helpful recommendations on how to motivate children in primary grades to learn science. They offer a wide range of activities, accompanied by photographs of children at work, that contribute greatly to an understanding of how to interest and involve children in science investigations.

Miles, Betty. *Save the Earth—An Ecology Handbook for Kids.* New York: Alfred A. Knopf, 1974.

The author presents to children a comprehensive view of the earth's ecological problems. She takes into account the integrative way children learn and combines reading skills, value learning, and concept formation throughout the book. The content is organized in sections: land, air, water, and how-to-do-it. Each section begins with an inspiring, informative background and well-chosen illustrations followed by projects that integrate all subjects of the curriculum. This is indeed a well-documented and creatively written ecology handbook for kids.

Milford, Susan. *The Kids' Nature Book.* Charlotte, VT: Williamson Publishing, 1989.

The book, organized for the year-round cycle, is written in calendar form and reflects seasonal changes.

It combines scientific explorations, art projects, and language (poems, stories, and write-ups) and focuses on nature and its phenomena, encouraging aesthetic appreciation and the conservation of nature.

It is written informally and can be used selectively. The content offers flexibility on how to adapt it developmentally, and the materials are found in nature. The activities can take place outside as well as inside the classroom.

A sourcebook for teachers and parents that emphasizes children's involvement and hands-on investigations.

Milgrom, Harry. *ABC Science Experiments.* New York: Crowell, 1970.

A brief, simple, colorful, easy to read series of 26 activities organized in an alphabetical sequence. It is written and illustrated for children, but an index of notes at the end of the book addresses adults and clarifies the science concepts that emerge from each investigation.

Mitchell, John Hanson. *A Guide to Seasons.* Lincoln, Mass.: Massachusetts Audubon Society, 1982.

This booklet is a selection of activities from the discontinued magazine *The Curious Naturalist* of the Massachusetts Audubon Society. The activities are organized by seasons as they appear in the Northern Hemisphere. They include all of nature's exhibits, such as animals, plants, the stars, and a weekly calendar of nature's events, such as which animals appear when and what flowers blossom when. It is heavily illustrated, well-documented, and informally written. An essential companion to a nature study that involves adults and children.

Munson, Howard R. *Science Activities with Simple Things.* Belmont, Calif.: Fearon Publishers, 1962.

This book of 29 experiments and 24 demonstrations was written as a supplement to any existing physical science program. The author specifies first the simple things and then designs activities that use them. The list of materials includes rubber bands, soda straws, paper clips, paper and plastic cups, marbles, boxes, pins and needles, and other odds and ends. The content of the book is divided into a series of experiments followed by demonstrations. The experiments are stated in terms of problems to be solved and include purpose, materials, procedure, and illustrations. The demonstrations are performed by teachers or students to explain a science fact or prove a point. The book will be useful to adults who understand science concepts and can capitalize on the availability of simple materials.

Nelson, Leslie, and George C. Lorbeen. *Science Activities for Elementary Children*. 8th ed. Dubuque, Iowa: Wm. C. Brown Publishers, 1984.

The book includes a very wide selection of activities for children in the elementary grades. The activities are organized thematically on the basis of physical, biological, and earth sciences. There are also interdisciplinary topics such as ecology, aviation, space travel, and health and safety. Each activity is stated as a problem, followed by recommended procedures and materials. The children's findings are suggested and the illustrations help the teacher to organize the investigations. A classic sourcebook of science activities in its eighth edition.

Nichols, Wendy, and Kim Nichols. *Wonderscience*. Palo Alto, Calif.: Learning Expo Publishing, 1990.

A developmentally appropriate series of activities in physical science. The topics are forces and movement, sound, air, water, and light.

The activities are described in lesson-plan formats; they provide open-ended questions and suggest variations for enrichment. They are accompanied by photographs that are helpful, mostly for teachers who hesitate to engage in physical science.

The activities can be used selectively and adapted to the early childhood program.

Furthermore, the presence of physical science in the young child's learning environment contributes to his or her construction of physical knowledge.

Nickelsburg, Janet. *Nature Activities for Early Childhood*. Reading, Mass.: Addison-Wesley, 1976.

The author, a long-time naturalist and educator, asks adults to "help children see more and not to obscure their vision with a multitude of facts." The 44 projects in nature activities are clearly stated, attractively illustrated, and encourage child involvement. Each project is independent, considers children's developmental stages, and provides adults with background material and vocabulary so they may facilitate the science experiences for the children. The activities are focused on animals, plants, and non-living things—all of which can be found in children's natural environments. The content is divided into various sections, such as outdoor group projects, projects with small animals, indoor projects, looking for things in the ground, watching things, and projects with plants. Each section ends with suggested books for adults and children. A valuable companion to the science curricula of preschool and early primary grades.

Ocone, Lynn, and Eve Pranis. *Guide to Kid's Gardening.* New York: John Wiley & Sons, 1990.

This "labor of love" originated with the National Gardening Association in 1983. Popular demand brought forth the publication in its present form. The book is written for parents, teachers, and youth leaders, so they may engage children of all ages in gardening tasks.

It offers basic tips on how to organize both indoor and outdoor gardening, develop sites, design gardens, and engage in planting.

A wide range of resources for adults and children is offered, as well as networking in the world of gardening. This is a sourcebook for the serious scholar of the science and art of gardening.

The Ontario Science Center. *Science Works.* Toronto, Canada: Kids Can Press, 1984.

The experiments in this sourcebook are organized under the titles The Science Show, The Great Outdoors, Puzzles and Mysteries, Energy Savers, Body Tricks, and Things to Make. Each hands-on experiment results in some visible phe-nomenon, followed by a paragraph that explains "how it works."

The drawings visually guide the reader in how to do the experiments.

For teachers, there is a wide selection of topics from which to choose to supplement a science curriculum. For parents, the book offers many opportunities to interact with their children through scientific experimentation.

Perdue, Peggy K. *Diving into Science.* Glenview, Ill.: Scott, Foresman & Co., 1990.

An activity book for children in the second to the fourth grade, it provides a hands-on learning opportunity for all students to get involved with water-related experiments. The content is organized under the headings: Water Experiments, Ocean-Going Vessels, Experiments Using Shells, Sand Experiments, and Labs Involving Ocean Animals.

The activities can be done in any sequence, and each is accompanied by a lab sheet containing questions with the expected right answers.

A learning-center approach is recommended as a teaching strategy to encourage independent learning. However, a teacher needs to have a good science background to support children's learning.

A bibliography on water and ocean-based science would have been helpful for the user of this book.

Perez, Jeannine. *Explore and Experiment.* Bridgeport, Conn.: First Teacher Press, 1988.

To achieve its affective and cognitive goals, this book emphasizes children exploring the environment in ways that result in knowledge and appreciation. Self-esteem is built into every activity, i.e., children's findings, thoughts, and feelings are taken seriously.

The book is organized in seven chapters: Introduction, Air, Water, Plants, Animals, Earth, and We All Do Our Part.

The book includes many recipes for materials that contribute to the explorations, such as cooking with clay, sand and casting, and a crystal garden.

The text is helpful to all teachers who care about the environment and practice structured but child-center strategies in their teaching. It is an appropriate sourcebook for parents, too.

Poppe, Carol A., and Nancy A. Van Matre. *Science Learning Centers for the Primary Grades*. West Nyack, N.Y.: Center for Applied Research in Education, 1985.

This book is organized with "hands-on," science-based activities and structured worksheets for the students to record their findings.

The science themes to be investigated are the five senses, the human body, space, plants, and dinosaurs.

The authors give teachers detailed directions on how to develop and manage a learning center, how to organize and plan each of the five topics, how to introduce the worksheets, and how to communicate to parents what the children are learning.

A helpful resource for the teacher who is thinking about developing and using learning centers as a teaching strategy.

Poppe, Carol A., and Nancy A. Van Matre. *K–3 Science Activities Kit*. West Nyack, N.Y.: Center for Applied Research in Education, 1988.

Five science units are included in this publication: weather, nutrition, birds, trees, and pets.

Each science unit is organized step by step with ready-to-use teacher-directed ideas.

The student follows directions to get desirable results and records findings in a preplanned worksheet. Each unit is followed by enrichment activities in which more child-centered initiatives are encouraged. The teacher is helped throughout this book with specific instructions on how to manage and teach activities, communicate to parents, and integrate skills from other subject areas.

Redleaf, Rhoda. *Open the Door Let's Explore*. St. Paul, Minn.: Toys 'n Things Press, 1983.

This book is a resource for parents and teachers who want to maximize young children's learning through the exploration of their physical environment. The author cautions adults on young children's developmental differences, emphasizes the integration of nature's exploration to the curriculum, elaborates on how learning may occur, and offers tips on how to develop effective walks. Each walk is independent and includes introductory activities, ideas for exploring, follow-up activities, language activities, and books for children. An informal, attractive resource book, easy to implement in any early childhood learning environment.

Richards, Roy. *An Early Start to Nature.* London, England: Macdonald Educational, 1989.

This publication has been widely circulated in the United States. It includes explorations of the natural world. The organization of the contents and the layout facilitate its use for teachers or parents of young children.

The activities are highlighted with drawings, pictures, children's work, and many practical tips on how to engage children in scientific investigations. They are developmentally appropriate and encourage and support children's initiatives. The book promotes the integration of other subjects such as mathematics, art, language, and appreciation of the environment.

Although it is not a guidebook, it weaves information on flowers, birds, fish, trees, and other aspects of nature into the suggested activities.

Richards, Roy. *An Early Start to Technology*. New York: Simon & Schuster, 1990.

Science and technology have strong links. Many times exploring the science that underlies the technology creates an exciting environment and conditions for children's learning.

This book engages children in exploring the effects of science on technology. The materials, such as ramps and a ball to explore forces, are simple. The illustrations contribute to the effectiveness of the content.

The book is appropriate for teachers or parents who are apprehensive about getting involved in science. The layout motivates adults to support children and their investigations. The hands-on, child-centered involvement makes it possible for children to construct their own understandings of how the materials interact with each other.

The goals are clearly stated: exploration, manipulation, observation, asking questions, testing, problem solving, and looking for patterns and relationships.

Richards, Roy, Margaret Collis and Doug Kincaid. *An Early Start to Science.* London, England: Macdonald Co., 1988.

An important contribution to the early childhood field from abroad.

This is a true primer, developmentally appropriate, and science-based sourcebook. It is useful to teachers and parents of young children and easy to adapt for children in the primary grades.

The content is based on the scenes from children's everyday lives and is presented in a visually effective way. The drawings and notations convey science concepts, teaching strategies, children's work, and ways to integrate it in the classroom.

The topics are: the senses, things that grow (i.e., plants), color, light, shadows, time (i.e., the duration of events), shells, stones and pebbles, bricks and blocks, seeds, fasteners, bottles and jars, toy animals, extensive resources for water play, outdoors, caring for dolls, flying things, electrical things, transparent things, and shiny things (reflections).

An explicit sourcebook, with a developmentally as well as a scientifically appropriate curriculum for young children.

Riegor, Edythe. *Science Adventures in Children's Play*. New York: Playschools Assoc., 1968.

This early pamphlet is sensitive and responsive to children's levels of interest and cognition. The science experiences are organized around topics such as exploring the neighborhood, map making, trees, birds, rocks and minerals, shadows and weather, wind, plants, animals, and ideas from here and there. Each investigation is integrated with other curriculum areas. The content is presented in a narrative form and includes information on the topic, suggestions on how to get started, how to involve children, and how to integrate each "adventure in science" with other curriculum areas. A helpful resource for a non-traditional classroom.

Rights, Mollie. *Beastly Neighbors*. Boston, Mass.: Little, Brown & Co., 1981.

This book is about exploring the "wild" world around you, whether urban or suburban, small town or big city. It provides many helpful tips on how to investigate your surroundings. For example, the supermarket is a science-based world whether you are at the produce, dairy, or meat department. Other topics explored are trees, weeds, ants, cockroaches and dinosaurs, a garden on the roof, air, rain, and recycling.

The style is a combination of narrative and illustrated directions on how to grow peanuts, how to run a snail race, and how to make mazes for mice, birdfeeders, leaf prints, dry flowers, and so forth. All activities are possible in the classroom environment. It is a great source for an after-school program, too.

Rockwell, Robert E., Elizabeth A. Sherwood, and Robert A. Williams. *Hug a Tree*. Mt. Rainier, Md.: Gryphon House, 1983.

This book gives information to parents and teachers on how to carry out environmental activities with children two to five years old. The information includes how to use language effectively and how to help children develop observation skills, identify, group, and record their findings. Furthermore, the logistics of organizing an outdoor experience are discussed in detail and supplemented with a list of books and other resources. Each activity designates age, cost of materials, what to do, and a "want to do more" section. Although each chapter is independent, it is advisable to use them in sequence. A book that is easy to integrate in a child-centered early childhood program.

Rose, Mary. *TREEmendous Activities for Young Learners.* Riverview, Fla.: Idea Factory, 1987.

This book offers a wide selection of activities to encourage children's investigations of trees. Objectives, materials, and strategies are very clearly stated and easily incorporated into the larger conceptual framework of a science curriculum; for example, changes in nature or extending a study on plant life.

Ross, Catherine, and Susan Wallace. *The Amazing Milk Book.* Reading, Mass.: Addison-Wesley Publishing Co., 1991.

An integrated approach to investigating milk and its implications in our lives. The two dozen projects incorporate many science-based activities. (The book is part of a series: *The Amazing Apple Book, Dirt Book, Paper Book,* and *Egg Book.*)

The book traces milk to its origins, explores how it gets to the carton, and discusses the various forms of milk that reach consumers.

The science-based activities are easy to implement and developmentally appropriate for a wide age range of children. A good supplemental resource in a curriculum on nutrition.

Rountree, Barbara S., Nancy Y. Taylor, and Melissa B. Shuptrine. *Where Are the Dinosaurs? Paleontology for Kids.* Tuscaloosa, Ala.: The Learning Line, 1989.

Although this sourcebook is for the elementary grades, it is rich in information, activities, and teaching strategies for children in their preschool years. The topic of dinosaurs is integrated into the curriculum and features a strong science component (anatomy, paleontology) and a process component (observation, comparisons, experimentation, predictions) of scientific thinking.

Children engage in activities that draw knowledge from paleontology. They simulate digs, observe the data on various dinosaurs, document their findings through language and art, relate them to the earth's geological epochs, and project them to their descendants.

With an abundance of resources for teachers, this comprehensive sourcebook on a topic of increasing interest to children offers a wide variety of opportunities for scientific investigations, as well as other creative pursuits.

Russell, Helen Ross. *Small World: A Field Trip Guide/Soil: A Field Trip Guide/Winter: A Field Trip Guide.* Boston, Mass.: Little, Brown & Co., 1972.

The three books in this series investigate in depth the environments of small living things, soil, and the season of winter, respectively. They present science information, along with teaching strategies for field trips. *Small World* explains habitats of insects, moss, lichens, etc., and helps teachers to organize discovery experiences for children outside the classroom. The content of *Soil: A Field Trip Guide* details a variety of rocks, minerals, dead plants, and animals, as well as the process of recycling. Ideas for projects on ecology are suggested for students to undertake. The exploration of a northeastern winter offers information on plants, birds, insects, ice, snow, and other aspects of nature's behavior during the winter season. A child-centered approach on how to engage children in investigations underscores the teaching strategy offered in this book. All three books are enhanced by excellent photographs and illustrations.

Russell, Helen Ross. *Ten Minute Field Trips—A Teacher's Guide*. Chicago, Ill.: J.G. Ferguson Publishing, 1973.

This book is written for children in the primary grades. Its focus is how to study the environment through ecological field trips on the schoolground or campground. The book is divided into sections on plants, animals, interdependence of living things, physical science, earth science, and ecology. Each section includes background material on the topic, related classroom activities, teacher preparation, and field trip possibilities. Furthermore, listings of field trips are cross-referenced for paved school grounds, and pictures are used widely to clarify sites and children's involvement. A widely used book for outdoor education.

Saul, Wendy, and Alan R. Newman. *Science Fare*. New York: Harper & Row, 1986.

This comprehensive book qualifies first as a guide to how and where children may engage in learning. It is also an exhaustive resource on where to find science and children's books, activities, and toys related to science learning. The lists are qualified with criteria on how to select them. The developmental differentiations and the quality of science included in the criteria are a valuable contribution for the teacher, parent, or youth leader who wants to develop a science-based activity.

The titles of the sections designate the content of this document: Science and Children's Literature; Getting Started with Science Things; Where to Buy What; Wild Wisdom; Biology Out of Doors; Magnifiers and Microscopes; To Better See You with My Dear!; Biology; Experimental Thinking; Digging Earth Science; Chemistry or Lex Luthor Doesn't Live Here;

Phasinating Physics; Astronomy; The Sky's the Limit; Wired for Electronics; A Computer Primer; and Building and Engineering, or, Look What I've Made.

This comprehensive reference-activity-guidebook is a must companion for the adult who is actively involved in the science education of children.

Schlichting, Sandi, and Marilyn Blackmer. *Super Science Sourcebook II*. Idea Factory, 1989.

The authors proclaim that hands-on science is important for learning about science and encourage teachers and parents to make it available, as well as to integrate it with math, language, social studies, and art.

The activities are divided by subject: Earth Science, Life Science, Physical Science, Science in the Library, Great Graphing, and Science Trivia.

The activities include objectives and procedures that direct children to experience phenomena and validate concepts and principles. At the end of each activity, there are questions that challenge children's thinking. Teachers who are knowledgeable about elementary science will be best qualified to use this resource.

Schmidt, Victor E., and Verix Rockcastle. *Teaching Science with Everyday Things*. 2nd ed. New York: McGraw-Hill, 1982.

The authors discuss their views on the importance of science for children and on the value of counting and measuring as process skills. Their emphasis is that process is as important as content; that in science, affective and cognitive objectives are equally important; and that materials of daily use are best suited for teaching science concepts. The authors address teachers with minimal science training and present them with science knowledge, as well as suitable teaching strategies. The illustrations enhance the explanations in the text and there is a categorized bibliography at the end of each chapter. This book goes beyond the scope of activities and is a useful resource for teachers.

Shaffer, Carolyn and, Erica Fidler. *City Safaris.* San Francisco: Sierra Club Books, 1987.

This urban ecology book encourages children to think of the city as a whole organism and to explore every aspect of the city so they can understand the "whole."

The explorations can be adapted to every age group, from four years old and up—from going around the block to finding out the routes traveled by tap water.

There are nine chapters: Shaping City Senses; Coping with Change; Creating Change; Neighborhood Adventures (1) City Streets, (2) City People; Heading Downtown; City Systems, How Does a City Get Enough to Eat? Taking Care of Leftovers; and Planning and Guiding Your Own Urban Safaris.

The strategies for explorations incorporate scientific thinking skills, as well as creativity and aesthetic appreciation.

Sheckles, Mary. *Building Children's Science Concepts. Experiences with Rocks, Soil & Water.* 3rd Printing. New York: Teachers College, Columbia University, Bureau of Publication, 1964.

Both a teacher training manual on how to organize good science training and an activities book on how to investigate the atmosphere, rocks, soil, and water. The author uses an open narrative style with suggestions on how children should investigate, discuss, and conceptualize science. A good resource for earth science curriculum in the primary grades.

Shermer, Michael. *Teach Your Child Science.* Los Angeles: Lowell House, 1989.

This book advises parents on how to get excited about and share with their children the wonders of science.

In Part I parents are told how being a scientist is part of being human and how children are natural scientists. Good advice is offered on how to interact with children on science issues and to understand the difference between science and pseudoscience.

In Part II—How to Engage in the Scientific Method—the importance of questioning and how to conduct experiments at home with your children are discussed.

It is more than a how-to book. Background knowledge is given on how to talk, think, and behave when you engage in scientific investigations. Seven appendixes provide lists of science books for parents and children; nature; science museums by region and state; how to create a tool kit; and scientific companies to contact for materials, magazines, and catalogues.

Sherwood, Elizabeth, Robert Williams, and Robert Rockwell. *More Mudpies to Magnets*. Mt. Rainier, MD: Gryphon House, 1990.

Over 120 science experiments are effectively organized for teachers. Each activity combines science content, the scientific method, easily found materials, and grade appropriateness (second to fifth).

The chapters are organized thematically: Chemistry Beginnings, First Physics, Earth Explorations, Weather Watchers, Flight and Space, All about Plants, Animal Adventures, and Hodge Podge.

A sourcebook to enrich any hands-on science curriculum.

Shuttleworth, Dorothy. *Exploring Nature with Your Child*. New York: Harry Abrams, 1977.

A narrative on nature, animals, and plants, accompanied by high-quality photographs, makes this book a valuable reference for classrooms, homes, camps, and wherever adults and children are engaging in nature study.

It will interest children of all ages. Younger ones will dwell on the pictures and listen to stories about them or make up their own. Older children may read about the animals, their habitats, life-styles, and how they protect themselves. Adults can also learn from this book and get ideas on how to explore and care for the environment, its inhabitants, and vegetation.

Silver, Donald M. *Life on Earth—Biology Today.* New York: Random House, 1983.

This reference book is particularly valuable for the colorful, explicit diagrams and excellent pictorial information on anatomical issues (the insides of a rabbit, for example) and on nature's processes, such as photosynthesis. The text is equally valuable to teachers and children in the primary grades. Plant and animal life is pictorially described with concrete explanations, and comparisons among organisms are creatively demonstrated. A valuable addition to any life sciences curriculum.

Sisson, Edith. *Nature with Children of All Ages.* Englewood Cliffs, N.J.: Prentice Hall, 1982.

This book is most suitable to share with children in exploring nature and teaching the outdoors. The author emphasizes the affective benefits of outdoors science investigations and offers concrete suggestions and tips on how to organize and plan these outings. Science background is offered to the adults, as well as teaching strategies on how to involve the children. The book is informal, direct, sensitive, and most valuable to teachers, parents, and camp leaders who want to investigate and enjoy nature with children. Attractive illustrations, informative diagrams, and a useful bibliography for both adults and children contribute to the effectiveness of this book.

Smith, Ellyn, Marilyn Blackmer, and Sandi Schlichting. *Super Science Sourcebook.* Riverview, Fla.: Idea Factory, 1987.

The activities in this science sourcebook encourage children's explorations. "Science education should be a journey not a destination" is one of the phrases used in the prologue.

The chapters are Earth Science Activities, Life Science Activities, Physical Science Activities, Intriguing Investigations, Kitchen Science Lab, Equipment You Can Make, Magic: Science in Disguise, Tracking Trivia, and E.T.C. (Every Topic Covered).

The science in this book is more appropriate for younger children (K–3).

The chapter on Intriguing Investigations presents process skills as a separate entity—more like a skill acquisition. However, all the activities can incorporate science process skills and combine the "journey" with the "destination."

Drawings and charts complement the activities.

Smith, Jamie C. *What Color Is Newton's Apple?* Monroe, N.Y.: Trillium Press, 1988.

A collection of activities in physics and chemistry for children (two to eight years). The activities are based on children's innate curiosity to "find out" and on assumptions that young children learn best through hands-on explorations of materials and phenomena.

The author emphasizes a child-centered approach through which the child "finds out" and talks about his or her findings. Furthermore, he sees great value in cooperative learning as a strategy for the children to exchange ideas. The teacher's role is to facilitate children's learning, development of thinking skills, problem solving, creativity, and communication.

Each activity includes age appropriateness, purpose, thinking skills, vocabulary, materials, and how to introduce, develop, and close the activity, and lists of questions to elicit desirable thinking and behavioral outcomes. Evaluation is a learning check-up procedure that is developmentally appropriate.

A sourcebook that combines theoretical constructs on how young children learn and the practice that elicits science-based learning.

The Smithsonian Institution. *Science Activity Book/ More Science Activities/ Still More Science Activities*. New York: G.M.G. Publishing, 1987, 1988, 1989.

All three books provide opportunities for families to engage in science-based activities. Families learning together can be creative in more than one way. The "hands-on," science-based activities relate to everyday life, utilize simple materials from the families' environments, and encourage adults and children to explore cooperatively.

The following selected activities demonstrate the scope of these action-oriented books: making cheese, trapping sun heat, crystal gardens, sound machines, ant farms, collecting and keeping worms in their newly constructed homes, 3–D viewers, and kaleidoscopes.

The directions are easy to follow, and the background knowledge given is appropriate to support the projects. Parents are cautioned not to "explain" and give answers, but to encourage questioning predictions and to keep the excitement in doing science-based projects.

The drawings enhance the publications greatly. The activities vary in their age appropriateness, so it is up to parents to make decisions based on children's ages and interests.

Sprung, Barbara, M. Froschl, and P.B. Campbell. *What Will Happen If. . . Young Children and the Scientific Method*. New York: Educational Equity Concepts, 1985.

The book emphasizes the importance of math, science, and technology-related activities to the development of young children. The spirit of inquiry and the equitable access by both sexes underscore the rationale and the strategies of implementation for a science program. The activities are organized around familiar surroundings and materials such as sand, water, blocks, and familiar machines, such as typewriters. Science concepts to explore include comparisons between water and sand; momentum with ramps and balls using the block area; density and viscosity using different liquids; and machines at home and school to explore technology. A brief but valuable chapter on resources complements this equitable approach to science experiences for young children of both sexes.

Stangle, Jean. *H2O Science*. Carthage, Ill.: Faron Teacher Aids, 1990.

This book contains science lessons and experiments using water for children in the elementary grades. Although the chapters have scientific headings (e.g., Buoyancy, Surface Tension), the activities are easy to do and the materials are simple and from our immediate environment. There is flexibility in the extent of the scientific investigation that can be conducted. Younger children may just explore, ask questions, and construct their own knowledge. Older children's questions and explanations will reflect more closely the actual science of the water.

Valid explorations are adaptable to any class, home, or outdoor environment that has access to water.

Stein, Sara. *Great Pets*. New York: Workman Publishing, 1976.

An Extraordinary Guide to Usual and Unusual Family Pets is the subtitle of the book and it is the most appropriate way to describe *Great Pets*. This book contains valuable information on a wide variety of animals that could be used as pets in schools and homes to enhance science teaching about animals. The author offers a wide variety of possibilities, with tips on cost, food, habitats, care, and brief summaries to help compare one animal with another in the same category. This information is grouped in the following categories: pets in the wild, overweight pets, vivarium pets, aquarium pets, serpentarium pets, pet birds, pocket pets, unusual apartment pets, pet cats, and pet dogs. A special section discusses and demonstrates the construction of various habitats. The illustrations and diagrams enhance even further this valuable companion to classrooms and homes that help children to raise and understand pets.

Stein, Sara. *The Science Book.* New York: Workman Publishing, 1979.

This unusual book encourages teachers (parents, too) and children to engage in investigations that concern their immediate environments, including themselves. The content is rich in science facts and ideas for investigation. It is divided into three sections: outsides, insides, and invisibles. These unusual categories address the types of investigations in which children may get involved. "Outsides" includes the behaviors of pests, pets, and people, and deals with topics like flea habits, baby and toddler behavior, and so forth. "Insides" addresses aspects of plants and animals that require probing, such as the assembly of children's skeletons, reproductive systems, and the nature of "goose pimples." "Invisibles" focuses on sensory experiences and perception. The investigations can be adapted for a wide range of ages and can also be integrated in the curriculum. The style is direct and informal, and the wide variety of photographs and diagrams contributes to the artistic appearance of this unusual, creative science book.

Stronck, David R., ed. *Understanding the Human Body. Sourcebook III.* Columbus, Ohio: ERIC/SMEAC, Ohio State University, 1983.

This well-organized sourcebook on the human body, its functions, health, growth, and development, contains 54 field-tested activities contributed by teachers of the elementary grades. The editor presents a convincing rationale for health education during the elementary schooling of children. The topics presented are body organs and systems, the five senses, growth and development, nutrition and foods, pollution, diseases and drugs, poisons, and safety. The activities for each topic are structured with a title, focus, background and challenges, materials and equipment, procedures, and further challenges and references. Each chapter is independent of the others, although a sequenced approach is recommended. The style is direct and informal and the activities are easy to implement. A valuable sourcebook for every classroom teacher.

Strongin, Herb. *Science on a Shoestring.* Reading, Mass.: Addison-Wesley Publishing, 1976.

This book aims to create low cost, high quality science for the elementary grades. The investigations are grouped around three conceptual themes: scientific methods, change and energy, and fields and forms. Each investigation follows a lesson plan and includes grade level, specific concept/skill, materials, vocabulary, activity, notes to teacher, approximate time duration, evaluation, and suggestions for extending the investigation at home. Although each activity is independent of the others, sequencing is recommended for certain of them, and the author cautions on differences of children's responses at different grade levels. The investigations can be integrated easily in a science curriculum where the process approach is essential.

Sund, Robert, B.W. Tillery, and L.W. Trowbridge. *Elementary Science Discovery Lessons: The Biological Sciences.* Boston, Mass.: Allyn and Bacon, 1970.

The investigations on animals and plants take into account the relationships of the organisms to their environments, their structures and function, and the diversity of type and unity of pattern in living things. Each investigation is organized to include grade level concepts, materials, procedure, teacher's questions for class discussion, and expected answers. A certain amount of background in biological sciences is recommended for the teacher.

Suzuki, David. *Looking at Plants*. New York: Warner Books, Inc., 1985.

This book provides hands-on experiments with seeds, roots, and plants in general, and examines soils and conditions for raising plants, edible and decorative plants, and how seasons affect plants. The drawings contribute greatly to the effectiveness of this book.

Suzuki, David. *Looking at Senses/ Looking at the Body/ Looking at Weather*. New York: John Wiley & Sons, 1986, 1987, 1988.

These paperback books with glossy, colorful covers are part of David Suzuki's "Looking at" series, published in the United States and abroad. They are a combination of "amazing facts" and hands-on investigations. Reflections on the topic investigated, challenging questions leading to the next investigation, awareness and appreciation of the natural world, and immediacy are how the author flows from one concept, thought, or feeling to another.

These texts are companions for a teacher, parent, or camp leader who is eager to learn more about science while working with children. They also qualify as children's books for fourth graders and up.

Looking at Senses explores the senses, their role, the organs, where they originate, and their dysfunctions, all of which are equally important for children to understand.

Looking at the Body addresses all aspects of the body and its functions and provides experiments for children to explore the body's various functions, including simulation of lungs and breathing. Health issues are integrated throughout the book.

Looking at Weather is an empowering book for understanding weather. Hands-on experiments using simple materials provide knowledge about some of the physical phenomena that affect the weather: hot and cold air, the water cycle, kites—anemometer for the wind, snowflake designs, temperature, even a cricket weather report!

Svezek, Sandra Histrom. *The World Around Us*. Lake Elsinore, Calif.: Pacific Shoreline Press, 1984.

The learning-center approach is based on the assumption that children learn most effectively when they engage in hands-on explorations using concrete materials, construct their own knowledge, make responsible choices, and become autonomous learners. The center designed by the teacher facilitates this learning through activities that are self-initiated and sustained by the children.

The topics to be taught are dinosaurs, rocks and fossils, desert and modern reptiles, mountains and forests, oceans, and space. Instructions on how to set up and develop a learning center are given. Photographs provide additional information, and the scientific investigations are integrated with language, art, and math.

A wide selection of resources accompanies each chapter. At the end of the book there are patterns from the outlines of animals that the teacher may reproduce to scale and the children may use in different ways.

Learning centers are gaining popularity among teachers.

Teaching Primary Science. 9 vols. Milwaukee, Wis.: Macdonald-Raintree, 1978.

These books represent joint efforts of scientists and teachers from many disciplines with a unified view on how children can learn science more effectively and enjoyably. Each book covers a specific topic and contains children's investigations, findings, and documentations, as well as the teachers' input in the actual teaching. Diagrams and photographs enhance further this valuable series on creative science teaching. The titles of the books in the series are: Candles, Seeds and Seedlings, Paints and Materials, Science from Water Play, Fibres and Fabrics, Mirrors and Magnifiers, Science from Wood, Musical Instruments, and Aerial Models.

Throop, Sara. *Science for the Young Child*. Belmont, Calif.: Fearon Publishers, 1974.

Although the author refers to this book as a "cookbook" with a variety of recipes to try, in reality it is more than that. A brief (61 Pages) but compact collection of science activities that are developmentally appropriate for young children (preschool-early grades) with topics that interest young children: senses, animal and plant life, weather, rocks, liquids, motion and movement, magnets, simple machines, and ourselves. Each topic is independent of the others. Tips are offered to teachers on how to facilitate children's learning. Interactions with materials and the articulation of children's findings are important learning objectives in this useful resource book for teachers of young children.

Ticotsky, Alan. *Who Says You Can't Teach Science?* Glenview, Ill.: Scott, Foresman & Co., 1985.

A combination of background information for teachers to show them that they can do science regardless of any educational background.

It includes three sections: (1) Materials of the Earth, (2) Physical Science (sound, light, color, simple machines, magnetism, and electricity), and (3) Plant and Animal Life.

The emphasis is on how to organize the classroom (set up a science center) and science investigations for the children.

Tilgner, Linda. *Let's Grow*. Pownal, VT: Storey Communications, 1988.

A hands-on gardening book with a wide range of background knowledge on the "science" of gardening, assumptions on how children learn, and instructional guidelines on how to engage the children in scientific explorations in an enjoyable way.

The book is divided into 13 chapters: The Child and the Garden, Gardening with Very Young Children, Gardening with

Children with Special Needs, Let's Dig! Tools to Fit, Let's Dig! Soil, Let's Plant! Vegetables, Let's Plant! Flowers and Herbs, Let's Plant! Trees, Let's Discover! Garden Helpers, Let's Discover! Nature's Gardens, Let's Discover! Plant Experiments, Let's Grow! Indoor Edibles, and Let's Grow! Houseplants.

A special table of contents gives listings of the appropriateness of projects for different age groups, as well as lists of projects by season.

The wide use of photographs further enhances this comprehensive publication on the benefits of nature's products to people's lives.

Ukeus, Leon (Ed.). *Science Experiences for Preschoolers—CES1 Sourcebook IV.* Columbus, OH: Clearing House for Science, Mathematics, and Environmental Education, 1986.

This sourcebook is valuable to teachers of young children. It is organized in four chapters.

1. The Introduction—theoretical constructs on what is science for young children.
2. General Activities—sensory explorations.
3. Life Science Activities—plants and animals.
4. Physical Science—water, sand, color, light, magnets, and static electricity.

The emphasis is on hands-on and developmentally appropriate investigations. Children's thinking is encouraged throughout the book.

UNESCO Sourcebook for Science Teaching. New York: UNESCO Publication Center, 1973.

The updated sourcebook on science experiments focuses on more formal science techniques and assumes that teachers must understand science. Although most of the activities are for older children, an experienced teacher can adapt some science experiments for children in the early grades. The content is organized around themes such as resources, facilities and techniques for science teaching, physical/biological science, and earth/space science. The appendixes include many scientific tables not applicable to the science learning of young children.

The Usborne Series of Science Books

The following publications originated in England, and their American editions have been widely circulated in the United States. They are reviewed as a group because of their common style and content.

Each book is written in a cartoon style, with illustrations that are a combination of lifelike and cartoonlike drawings. The written parts are either in captions or in self-contained paragraphs. Inviting to children. They are grouped according to the publishers' intended series.

1. Usborne Explainers
   a. *Things that Fly*
   b. *Things that Float*
   c. *Things on Wheels*
   Tulsa, Okla.: EDC Publishing, 1987.

Each booklet is effectively illustrated with the corresponding variety of "things" we use in transportation. The language is precise and informative and written for a wide range of ages. Teachers may read them to younger children and share the pictures, while older children may do both on their own.

2. Usborne First Science
   a. *Science Surprises*
   b. *Science Tricks and Magic*
   c. *Weighing and Measuring*
   London, England: Usborne Publishing (American edition), 1986.

Each booklet is written in a cartoon style and sequence, with appropriate captions describing the experiments and explaining the science that relates to them. The colors, characters, and action are appealing to children and developmentally appropriate for children in the primary and elementary grades.

3. Usborne Science Activities
    Science with Magnets
    London, England: Usborne Publishing, 1990.

This 24–page booklet is overwhelmingly rich in activities based on magnets and is colorful and inviting to children, as well as to teachers. It is organized under the headings What Can a Magnet Do? Pulling Power, Pulling Through, Pushing and Pulling, Finding Your Way, Making Magnets, Around Your Magnet, Electricity and Magnets, Electromagnets, and Magnets and Machines—and includes a series of explanations to facilitate children's understanding as they engage in these activities.

4. Usborne Starting Point Science
    a. *What Makes it Rain?*
    b. *What's Underground?*
    c. *What Makes a Flower Grow?*
    d. *Where Does the Electricity Come From?*
    Tulsa, Okla: EDC Publishing, 1986, 1987, 1988, 1989.

All four booklets are bright and exciting for children. The information included is depicted in illustrations that challenge children to ask questions and seek answers. The booklets can be used as supplements to hands-on investigations.

5. Usborne Science and Experiments
    a. *The World of the Microscope*
    b. *Ecology*
    London, England: Usborne Publishing, 1987, 1988.

The projects and activities backed by sound science information and written in the distinct Usborne style are more appropriate for children in the upper elementary grades.

6. Usborne Pocket Scientist
   a. *Flight and Floating*
   b. *Chemistry Experiments*
   c. *Fun with Electronics*
   London, England: Usborne Publishing, 1981.

These colorful pocket-size books are full of experiments and projects that contribute to children's understanding of scientific principles.

Fun with Electronics provides instructions (illustrated) for making a radio that are appropriate for children in the upper elementary grades.

Watson, Philip. *Light Fantastic/Amazing Air/Super Motion/Liquid Magic.* New York: Lothrop, Lee & Shepard Books, 1982.

A series of illustrated activities books that provide explicit information on how to engage children in science-based explorations that lead to discoveries. Each book (approximately 45 pages) is organized conceptually; for example, *Light Fantastic* introduces the teacher to basic materials that are needed to explore light. The headings of each series of investigations are Power of Light, Mirror Images, Colour, Artificial Light, Tricks of Light, Light and Shadow; and each book contains a glossary.

The activities can be used selectively. Some are more appropriate for younger children, and others are more appropriate for older children. The publications are very inviting to children and can supplement any hands-on science curriculum in which children are encouraged to make their own discoveries.

Webster, David. *Exploring Nature Around the Year: Spring/Summer/Autumn/Winter*. Englewood Cliffs, N.J.: Julian Messner, 1990.

This book presents seasonal activities based on science. Although they are related to nature, many of the activities and projects can be done in the classroom.

The activities are child-centered, hands-on investigations using scientific skills, such as observations, comparisons, predictions, and experimentation. Tips on how to document findings are given. Unified themes, such as the weather and nature's changes, are studied, interrelated, and recorded throughout the seasons.

Westley, Joan. *Windows on Beginning Science—Active Learning for Young Children*. 6 vols. Sunnyvale, Calif.: Creative Publications, 1988.

The science program features a hands-on approach to science learning and is developed especially for children in grades K–2.

Each book can be used independently as a resource for engaging children in science-based investigations. The topics of each book are

1. Seeds and Weeds
2. Insects and Other Crawlers
3. Rocks, Sand, and Soil
4. Water and Ice
5. Constructions
6. Light, Color, and Shadows

A separate management guide includes strategies, recordkeeping, storage tips, safety guidelines, and detailed descriptions of scientific skills and how they apply to each topic and lesson. Worksheets are available to assist children in keeping records of their findings.

Each investigation (identified as a "window") involves a detailed analysis on how to engage children in finding out about the concept under investigation. For example, an investigation in comparing beans would include identifying the objective, initiating the activity, guiding children's actions (including what questions to ask), and, finally, suggestions for extending the activities.

The activities are integrated with math, art, language, and social studies, when appropriate.

Wheatley, John, and Herbert Coon. *100 Teaching Activities in Environmental Education.* Columbus, Ohio: Ohio State University, The ERIC Center for Science, Mathematics, and Environmental Education, 1970.

A well-documented resource for teachers of children of all ages. The color-coded pages divide the book into grade levels (K–3, 4–6, 7–9, 10–12). Although the activities address environmental science, other subject areas are effectively integrated in the investigations. Each activity includes grade level, subjects (other than science), problems to be investigated, concept, purpose of the activity, references, and the activity itself, with tips on how to enhance further children's learning. The style is direct and informal, provides excellent organization, and the book is a valuable resource for teachers of environmental education.

Wilkes, Angela. *My First Nature Book.* New York: Alfred A. Knopf, 1990.

This is another 10" x 13" hard-cover book that invites adults and children to explore the wonders of nature, interspersed with photographs that clarify the suggested investigations and projects.

The ideas may be familiar, but the way in which they are articulated is not.

The contents of the book are organized as follows: Nature in Pictures, Nature Spotter's Kit, A Nature Museum—Nature Showcase, Collecting Seeds—Sprouting Seeds—Watching Seeds Grow, Feeding the Birds—Birds' Menu, Tree Prints, From Bud to Leaf, Creepy Crawly Pit-Traps, A Battle Garden—World in a Bottle, Caterpillar House—From Caterpillar to Butterfly, Flower Press, Everlasting Flowers, A Worm Farm, Petwatching, Tracking Your Pets, Your Nature Diary, and Country Code.

All in 48 pages!

Wilkes, Angela. *My First Science Book.* New York: Alfred A. Knopf, 1990.

This 10" x 13" hard-cover book is an inviting initiation to science. The emphasis on color, high-quality paper, and a color-coded, illustrated table of contents will convince even the most reluctant adult or child to get involved in science. A "how to use this book" section helps you proceed step by step through each experiment in your kitchen or classroom.

Desirable results are shown in life-size pictures and the colorfulness of the content makes it hard to resist. It is hoped that the reality of the experience in which children are engaged will fuel their curiosity to continue their investigations beyond what the book provides.

Wilkes, Angela, and David Mostyn. *Simple Science.* London, England: Usborne Publishing, 1983.

This colorful book, full of illustrations in cartoon-like style that challenge and informative content, is an invitation to adults and children to engage in science investigations. It addresses all developmental stages and encourages hands-on involvement. The questions probe children's observational skills and challenge their thinking.

Topics included in the text are Science All Around You, Air is Real, Hot Air, Vanishing Water, Water in the Air, Special Effects with Water, Does Water Have a Skin? Floater and Sinker, Shadowplay, Reflections, Coloured Light, Why do Things Make Sounds? What is Gravity? Bounces and Springs, Simple Machines, Magnetic Powers, and Crackles and Sparks; the book also contains a glossary.

Williams, Robert, Robert Rockwell and Elizabeth A. Sherwood. *Mudpies and Magnets.* Mt. Rainier, MD: Gryphon House, Inc., 1988.

This book consists of 112 hands-on activities, easy to implement in the classroom. Each activity provides science content for the teacher, a teaching strategy (which includes the scientific method), easy-to-find materials, and is age appropriate (preschool to second grade).

The chapters are organized as follows: On Your Own, Science Center Activities, Building with Science, Constructions and Measurement, Science for a Crowd, Circle Time Activities, Paints and Prints, Scientific Art, Wet and Messy, Science for a Special Place, Science to Grow On, Health and Nutrition, Learning About Nature, Act Out, Science in a Big Way, Creativity and Movement, and Hodge Podge.

The diversity in content and the brief comments on each activity demonstrate the many possibilities of how to integrate science into the curriculum.

Willow, Diane, and Emily Curran. *Science Sensations: An Activity Book from the Children's Museum, Boston.* Reading, Mass.: Addison-Wesley Publishing Company, 1989.

This book of hands-on explorations in the physical world reflects the viewpoint of the author that children construct their own knowledge as they act upon materials and observe phenomena.

The topics under investigation are part of our everyday life: Light, Color, Shadows, Reflections, Water, Wind, Balance, Illusions, Moving Pictures, and Patterns.

These investigations engage the child in experiments that lead them to their findings. Proposals on how to go further follow each investigation.

The drawings of children represent diversity and the photography is both artistic and scientific.

Woodward, Carol, and Robert Davitt. *Physical Science in Early Childhood.* Springfield, Ill.: Charles C. Thomas, Publisher, 1987.

This book combines teacher training with activities.

The first part sets up all the theoretical assumptions on how children learn at different developmental levels and how the physical aspects of the world contribute to the hands-on exploration and construction of knowledge for the children.

The authors propose materials, develop the constructs on their appropriateness, describe the teacher's supportive role, and discuss how skillful questioning encourages children's development in scientific thinking. The activities model in practice all the theory and are explicit on how to engage children and encourage them to do investigations and test out their assumptions. The photography complements the written part.

The physical science experiences are described under the headings Blowing, Pushing Pulling, Pendulum, Projecting, Rolling, Balancing, Tying, and Shadows. All headings suggest interactive involvement in the physical aspects of the world around us.

Wyler, Rose. *Science Fun with Toy Boats/ Science Fun with Peanuts/ Science Fun with Mud and Dirt.* New York: Julian Messner, 1986.

A combination of story-telling and activities designed to illustrate the theme of each story.

The activities are applications of scientific principles, and the explanations inform how the principle and the activity are related.

The drawings enhance the text, and it is easy to follow directions for such activities as making boats out of milk bottles.

The author recommends these books for classrooms and for children at home.

Zubrowski, Bernie. *Ball Point Pens/ Bubbles/ Milk Cartons/ Water Pumps.* Boston, Mass.: Little, Brown Co., 1979.

Zubrowski, Bernie. *Wheels at Work/ Raceways/ Clocks.* New York: William Morrow Co., 1986.

Zubrowski, Bernie. *Tops.* New York: Morrow Junior Books, 1989.

These books do not fall into any traditional category of activity books, but they capture the essence of what science for young children ought to be. Each topic is only the starting point for exploring concepts through manipulation, construction, and interaction, so that children may understand and appreciate the wonder of science.

They are valuable resources for teachers and parents who understand the importance of young children's learning. The most celebrated of the books is *Bubbles,* a valuable addition to the water tables in early childhood learning environments.

IV

Science Books for Young Children

Miriam Marecek
Boston University

Never before has there been such a rich supply of non-fiction books available for young children! The use of color, photography, narrative, and fictional texts to explore and describe the wonders of this world, both above us and beneath our feet, has been inspiring. Books that excite, explore, and dazzle the curious and inquisitive minds of young children are sprouting up in a variety of unusual formats faster than I can read them. For the past decade, there has been a strong, steady growth in all children's books. Thanks to thematic curriculum units, as well as literature-based reading programs, there has been a tremendous increase in the variety of books published for the young child. Many teachers of young children have used books in their classrooms, both as resources for investigations as well as to spark new interests. Parents, concerned with surrounding young children with quality materials, are buying books and building home libraries. What to select, what are the "best" books on each topic, and what is most appropriate developmentally are concerns for all of us who want the very best for young children everywhere.

The changes in informational literature have been truly significant in the past several years—so much so that some of the old criteria no longer apply. Children who thrive on questions need books that foster their inquisitiveness, their curiosity, and their wonder. Books that kindle their excitement and nurture their openness to new ideas and interests are what will help to make children scientifically literate.

These are some criteria that I used in the final selections:

1.   Books that frame accurate information in a story format.

In this appropriate story, *Feathers for Lunch*, Lois Ehlert masterfully opens up the doors to the balance of nature with the "lunch that got away." There is an element of tension as the cat searches for birds for her lunch, as well as a sense of humor and relief as we look carefully at all the birds—"the lunch that got away."

> A book is the beginning of an exploration, and that exploration shouldn't end on the last page of the book. It should be open ended enough so that children can pursue things beyond what is immediately on the page.

So says Lois Ehlert, whose nature-inspired books provide us with both a feast for the eyes and food for thought. A glance at her brightly colored books gives one an impression of her varied style and creative formats. Even the jackets of the books are used creatively to include a checklist of birds or, on another book, a recipe for vegetable soup. "I hate to hit kids over the head with information, yet I try to include as much of it as I can," she adds. *Feathers for Lunch* is notable not only for its bold art work, but also because the non-fiction (drawings and life-size detail of birds) and the fiction (a rhymed story about the cat and his inability to catch the birds) are intertwined so that a new vision of the informational book is formed. No longer is information presented in a narrative that is good for reference but boring for sharing. *Feathers for Lunch* will pique every child's curiosity with its rich ingredients of fact and fiction. It is a splendid example of merging story and fact.

2. Books that integrate illustrations and narration well.

Some books, like *The Salamander Room*, can actually, through a web of inferences and the simplicity of their words, create a poetic feeling relevant to the young child's experience and background. "Where will he sleep? Where will he play?" asked Brian's mother as he brought home a small, orange salamander and tenderly cared for him, considering his needs. Purposeful integration of narration and illustrations can enhance the use of books for science.

3. Books that are relevant to young children's experiences.

There are plenty of information books on every topic, available in intriguing new formats that are visually striking. "The Eyewitness Series," especially the paperback series "The Eyewitness Junior Books," published by Knopf, center around a close-up photograph on each full-page spread intertwined with sketches and fascinating details that are especially appealing to children. The aim of this wonderful series is to excite new interests but not "overkill" with too much information. *Amazing Cars, Amazing Animal Disguises, Amazing Armored Animals*, and *Amazing Frogs and Toads* are some of the outstanding new titles. As soon as they can, young children will rush to read the bigger Eyewitness Books on the topic of their choice. They will pore over these books for endless hours.

4. Books that demonstrate facts with hands-on evidence and give children clear opportunities to check things out for themselves.

Perhaps the most intriguing new books for young scientists are the "First Discovery Series" translated from the French and published by Scholastic in their "Cartwheel Series." In brilliant color, vivid images spring to life, all with the turn of brightly printed, transparent pages. We can see a chick grow inside an egg and then hatch, as well as a tree change through the seasons. We can observe a ladybug lay eggs on a leaf almost right before our eyes. These books contain a bit of surprise and wonder, which intrigues children of all ages.

5. *Books that have a depth and appropriateness of content.*

Two great examples of the depth of a topic are Charles Micucci's *The Life and Times of An Apple* and Clare W. Leslie's *Nature All Year Long.*

Both books give readers fresh approaches to information. Charles Micucci's concise text is enhanced by over 100 finely detailed, full-color illustrations, as well as interesting tid-bits about apples that young children will especially want to know. "An apple a day keeps the doctor away" is an old saying based on the nutritional qualities of the apple. Another page gives clear descriptions in words, with fine illustrations, of the varieties of domestic apples available in the United States. In her book, *Nature All Year Long,* Claire Walker gives intricate and helpful hints for looking at nature throughout the year. These include things to do and to make. This is a treasure chest of a month-by-month journal of hibernating animals and changing trees and shrubs, as well as a glance at marine creatures and weather. Carefully sketched with lively drawings, this is an inspiring guide for young children who seem to know inherently that each month and each season has its own time clock. We are fortunate to have books of such depth to nurture young children.

6. *Books that display a unique organization, with a clearly written format.*

Two series, "Eye Openers" and the "Look Closer" books published by Dorling Kindersley, exhibit a unique format. Large, detailed illustrations span both pages and a simple text satisfies young, inquiring minds. Small, close-up views of parts of the animal are featured on each page; details of the teeth or the tail are especially interesting to young children. Some great titles are: *The Body and How It Works, Birds and How They Live,*

Rainforest, Desert Life, and *Pond Life.* Their series for the youngest explorers on such topics as birds, insects, flowers, and weather, deserve a "closer look." Still another group of books published by Dorling Kindersley, called "What's Inside?," focus on plants, insects, boats, and babies.

My First Green Book, another welcome series with simple, easy-to-follow, step-by-step instructions for experiments and life-size photographs of everything you need, is truly a fine example of unique organization. Everyone can learn to cook with *My First Cook Book* and *My First Baking Book,* or try to do fascinating experiments with *My First Science Book.*

Red Leaf, Yellow Leaf, by Lois Ehlert, exemplifies unique organization, as the book shows the growth of a maple tree from seed to sapling. Brilliant collages, aesthetic cut-outs, and careful research—giving the adult readers more information in tiny print in the front and back of the book—and keeping the young child in mind throughout the text, is an example of the best for young children.

7. *Books that focus with integrity on different viewpoints.*

The Usborne Series, written on almost every major topic of interest to children, focuses on a variety of topics with integrity. Text and pictures are interlaced in a unique format that children enjoy. Over 60 titles on 50 different subjects, ranging from *Where Rubbish Goes* to *Science in the Kitchen,* have been published.

Another example of a scientifically accurate book with a different viewpoint is *My Place in Space,* by Robin and Sally Hirst, which gives children a glimpse of their home in relation to the hemisphere, the planet, and the solar system.

8. *Books that create an irresistible enthusiasm for the topic.*

JoAnna Cole and Bruce Degen have intrigued children with their "Magic Schoolbus Series" (Scholastic) and have enlivened such topics as water purification, the solar system, inside the human body, and inside the earth. Their accurate and carefully presented facts, juxtaposed with a zany teacher and lively class, give the children information in multi-variety levels. Often children at different age levels can read these books together and concentrate on the variety of information packed on each page. This information is accurately presented and not undermined by the humorous portrayal of a wacky teacher.

Yoshi's *Who's Hiding Here?* explores animal camouflage through exquisite die-cut pages of magnificent batik paintings. A rhythmic text and a game-like format is a creative introduction to our environment.

The Cousteau Society's *Turtles* (Little Simon Books) explores the life cycle and behavior of a green turtle through exquisite photographs. Aladdin's "Early Reader Pop-Up Books" give young children unforgettable views of their favorite topic, dinosaurs.

There is an element of real joy in poring over these new books—the joy of discovery, the joy of being alive, the joy of nurturing nature. In many of these books, there is the awareness of the miracle of life and the wonder of exploration. It is a feeling that the master writer E.B. White captured so well in *Charlotte's Web* when he wrote:

> Life in the barn was very good—night and day, winter and summer, spring and fall, dull days and bright days. It was the best place to be, thought Wilbur, this warm delicious cellar, with the garrulous geese, the changing seasons, the heat of the sun, the passage of swallows, the nearness of rats, the sameness of sheep, the love of spiders, the smell of manure, and the glory of everything.

As educators, it is our job to give all children everywhere new dimensions to their lives. What better way to begin than to spark their curiosity and delight in their explorations by surrounding them with wonderful books.

The following annotated selections have been made with great care, for it is a primary task and challenge of teachers, parents, and all those who work with the young, to provide carefully about which science books are most appropriate for your child's developmental level and which ones will delight him or her, for *you* are the ultimate matchmaker between a book and a child. Turn your child on to the wonder of science through these marvelous books.

REFERENCES

Cartwheel Series. First Discovery Books. Topics include Bears, The Tree, Airplane and Flying Machines, Earth and Sky, Weather, and The Lady Bug. New York: Scholastic, 1991.

Cole, JoAnna. *Inside the Human Body/ Inside the Earth/ Lost in the Solar System/On the Ocean Floor.* The Magic Schoolbus Series. New York: Scholastic, 1990, 1989, 1990, 1992.

The Cousteau Society. *Turtles.* Little Simon Books, 1992.

Early Reader Pop-Up Books Series. New York: Aladdin, 1990.

Ehlert, Lois. *Red Leaf, Yellow Leaf/ Feathers for Lunch.* New York: Harcourt Brace Jovanovich, 1991, 1990.

Eye Openers Series. Topics include Colors, Planes, Pets, Dinosaurs, Sea Animals, and Reptiles. New York: Aladdin, 1992.

Eyewitness Junior Books Series. Topics include Amazing Mammals, Amazing Bears, and Amazing Lizards and Birds. New York: Knopf, 1992.

Hirst, Robin, and Sally Hirst. *My Place in Space.* New York: Orchard, 1988.

Leslie, Clare W. *Nature All Year Long.* New York: Greenwillow, 1991.

Mazer, Anne. *The Salamander Room.* New York: Knopf, 1991.

Micucci, Charles. *The Life and Times of the Apple.* New York: Orchard, 1992.

Taylor, Barbara. *Pond Life.* Look Closer Series. New York: Dorling Kindersley, 1992.

Usborne Books. *Science in the Kitchen/ Where Rubbish Goes.* Tulsa, Okla.: EDC, 1992.

Wilkes, Angela. *My First Green Book/ My First Cook Book/ My First Baking Book.* New York: Knopf, 1991.

Wilkes, Angela. *My First Science Book.* New York: Knopf, 1990.

Yoshi. *Who's Hiding Here?.* Needham, Mass.: Picture Book Studio, 1987.

Some excellent sources for science book reviews:

"The Kobrin Letter," a newsletter published by Beverly Kobrin, costs $12 and is published ten times annually. To order, write to 732 N. Greer Road, Palo Alto, CA 94303.

Appraisal, a professional journal specifically designed to evaluate science books for children, is published three times a year by Boston University, 605 Commonwealth Avenue, Boston, MA 02215. It has a unique format. Each book is reviewed by both a children's librarian and a science specialist in the field, and often they do not agree. These reviews provide some lively reading!

BIBLIOGRAPHY

A Closer Look

Branley, Franklyn M. *Gravity Is a Mystery.* New York: Harper Collins, 1986.

Wonderful, lively story which explains the concept of gravity.

Eye-Opener Series on *Trains, Trucks, Diggers and Dump Trucks.* New York: Aladdin Books/Macmillan Publishers, 1992.

Superb close-up photographs help satisfy inquisitive questions from young children about things that go.

Goor, Ron, and Nancy Goor. *Shadows: Here, There, and Everywhere.* New York: Crowell, 1981.

The authors use simple words and photos to explain how shadows are formed.

Hoban, Tana. *Look Up, Look Down.* New York: Greenwillow, 1991.

Photographs that present objects and scenes from different perspectives, some viewed from below and some viewed from above.

Hoban, Tana. *Shadows and Reflections.* New York: Greenwillow: 1992.

Unique photographs without text feature shadows and reflections of various objects, animals, and people.

Let's Explore Science Series. *Make It Change, Make It Go* (learn about energy using household equipment). *Make It Balance* (gravity). New York: Dorling Kindersley, 1992.

Lively questions and clear action photographs are combined to help a child investigate how "physics" and "chemistry"—dissolving, freezing, decaying, and evaporation—all involve the conversion of energy. This series enables children to experiment with a range of materials and processes including heating, cooling, stirring, staining, and soaking.

All About Animals

Arnold, Caroline. *Cheetah/Hippo/Kangaroo/Koala,* among others in this fine series. New York: Morrow Junior, 1992. Photographs by Richard Hewett.

This exceptional series of animal books has won many awards, especially the Outstanding Science Trade Book Award for Children. Very fine photographs of close-ups of animals that will intrigue the younger children.

Banks, Merry. *Animals of the Night.* Illustrated by Ronald Himler. New York: Scribner's, 1990.

A warm story about night animals, including opossums, coyotes, porcupines, and skunks, combined with Ronald Himler's luminous watercolor illustrations, creates a very special picture book.

Cole, JoAnna. *Large As Life Animals.* Illustrated by Kenneth Lily. New York: Knopf, 1985.

Brief text and breath-taking, life-size illustrations present the characteristics of diurnal and nocturnal animals for young children.

Feldman, Eve B. *Animals Don't Wear Pajamas: A Book About Sleeping.* Illustrated by Mary Beth Owens. New York: Holt, 1992.

Hummingbirds, elephants, octopuses, lions, gorillas, puffin, warthogs, lizards, dolphins, grey wolves, sea otters, and snow leopards . . . also includes what these animals do when they are awake!

George, William T. *Box Turtle at Long Pond.* Illustrated by Lindsay Barrett George. New York: Greenwillow, 1989.

In a gentle, almost story-like format with detailed illustrations, a box turtle searches for food, basks in the sun, and escapes from a raccoon on the shore of Long Pond. Follows another beautiful nature book, *Beaver at Long Pond.*

Howes, Jim. *A Place for Them All.* Illustrated by Annette Dowd. New York: Simon & Schuster, 1987.

Presents different ways animals find and make their homes in caves, trees, underground, and in the ocean, as well as activities for making homes in your backyard.

Kitchen, Bert. *Somewhere Today.* Cambridge, Mass.: Candlewick Press, 1992.

"Somewhere today, a spotted skunk is performing a handstand" or "two brown hares are boxing." Young children are intrigued by dramatic animal behaviors. Small print gives a "nutshell" background for adult readers.

Loewer, Peter. *The Inside-Out Stomach.* Illustrated by Jean Jenkins. New York: Atheneum, 1990.

Describes the physical characteristics and natural environment of a variety of animals that do not have backbones, including amoebas, other one-celled animals, and worms. Accurate black and white drawings illustrate these fascinating creatures.

McDonnell, Janet. *Animal Communication.* Chicago: Children's Press, 1989.

Examines forms of animal communication, including alarm signals, indications of territory, and mating rituals.

McGrath, Susan. *Saving Our Animal Friends.* Washington, D.C.: National Geographic, 1986.

Concern and awareness of current issues involving endangered species is presented in a color photo essay. Sparse text enhances the visual effect of the book.

Parsons, Alexandra. *Amazing Poisonous Animals.* Photographs by Jerry Young. The Eyewitness Juniors Book Series. New York: Knopf, 1990.

Richly captured photographs introduce poisonous animals such as the fire salamander, the gila monster, the death puffer, and the sea anemone. The photographs' texture encourages the child to touch the page, but, of course, not the real animal.

Pearce, Q.L. *Animal Footnotes.* Illustrated by Delana Bettoli. Eden Prairie, Minn.: Silver Press, 1991.

From antelopes to zebras, this book focuses on animal locomotion. Footprints of 40 animals and facts about their feet, speed, and travel habits will intrigue children and encourage them to move the way animals do.

Riha, Susanne. *Animals in Winter.* Minneapolis, Minn.: Carolrhoda, 1989.

Some of the hibernating creatures you'll meet in this book include the marmot, the hedgehog, and even the garden snail.

Detailed illustrations will help young children learn about different ways these animals prepare for the winter and how they survive through the cold months.

Royston, Angela. *Night Time Animals*. Eye Opener Series. New York: Aladdin/Macmillan, 1992.

Large photographs and a clear, concise text describe some animals that are active at night such as foxes, bats, and owls.

Shepard, Elizabeth. *No Bones*. Illustrated by Ippy Patterson. New York: Macmillan, 1988.

With this book you can identify creepy crawlies, animals with no bones or invertebrates. A good teacher's guide, as well as a resource book for the older child. Usually shows two pictures of animals side by side, the larger drawing depicting how the animal might look under a magnifying glass.

Taylor, Kim. *Hidden By Darkness*. New York: Doubleday Dell, 1990.

Creatures of the night come alive in this color photographic essay. Mysterious night noises, eyes in the dark, and snails' slime are ideas that will captivate children.

van der Meer, Ron, and Atie van der Meer. *Amazing Animal Senses*. Boston: Little, Brown, 1990.

A superb interactive book, including three-dimensional pictures that encourage all five human senses to participate in learning about animals. For example, looking through the eyes of an owl and trying to catch a mouse before it escapes into its hole are some of the activities incorporated in the book.

Animals: Camouflage

Amazing Animal Disguises. Eyewitness Junior Series. New York: Alfred A. Knopf, 1992.

How does an opossum pretend to be dead? A fascinating book in an innovative series that shows close-up photos of the marvels and mysteries of animal disguises.

Dewey, Jennifer. *Can You Find Me?* New York: Scholastic, 1989.

How animals survive in their natural surroundings fascinates young children. Readers will encounter mammals, reptiles, and insects and will witness their camouflaging adaptations through the excellent drawings of naturalist Jennifer Dewey.

Wood, John Norris. *Nature Hide & Seek:* OCEANS. New York: Knopf, 1985.

Lurking in weeds, concealed in darkness, and buried in sand, fascinating creatures of the sea are camouflaged in coral reefs. Through the fold-out flaps, you can dive in and discover nature's strangest and most wonderful creatures. A unique format that would add to any ocean display.

Yoshi. *Who's Hiding Here?* Needham, Mass.: Picture Book Studio, 1987.

A rhyming text explores animal camouflage through batik on silk illustrations. Die-cut pages reveal the animals hiding throughout the book. Exquisitely designed, this book is a treasure to explore with young children. Scientific notes on the back pages give an in-depth explanation of specific animal adaptations.

Animals: Eggs

Hariton, Anca. *Egg Story.* New York: Dutton, 1992.

With charming illustrations, architect and painter Anca Hariton tells the story of the egg. Each stage is carefully presented in the world of the farmyard. A first science book for the youngest.

Jeunesse, Gallimard, and Pascale de Bourgoing. *The Egg.* Illustrated by P.M. Valet. The Cartwheel Book Series. New York: Scholastic, 1992.

Originally published in France, these unique spiral-bound books, with plastic overlays, are truly magic. You can "look directly into an egg, an apple, a tree, a flower . . . all with the turn of a brightly painted transparent page."

Other titles in the series include *Colors*, *Fruit*, *The Ladybug and Other Insects*, *Weather*, and *The Tree*.

Lauber, Patricia. *What's Hatching Out of That Egg?* New York: Crown, 1979.

Striking black and white photographs enhance a well-researched text that draws on clues to reveal the birth of 11 different animals that hatch from eggs—from spiders to ostriches.

Selsam, Millicent. *Egg to Chick*. Illustrated by Barbara Wolff. New York: Harper & Row, 1970.

A timeless book from the special I Can Read series that depicts how an egg grows into a chicken in 21 days.

Turner, Dorothy. *Eggs*. Illustrated by John Yates. Minneapolis, Minn.: Carolrhoda, 1989.

Touches upon everything you would want to know about eggs, including cooking hints on how to boil an egg or make a sweet souffle omelet, as well as the role eggs play in various cultures. A well-rounded book on this topic.

Animals: Farm

Farm Animals: An Eye Openers Book. Photographs by Philip Dowell. New York: Aladdin, 1991.

Sheep, ducks, pigs, and goats are among the close-ups in this Eye Openers book. Historical illustrations, along with the usual stunning visuals, help illuminate the importance of these animals today as in earlier times. A book young children will pore over for hours.

Fischer-Nagel, Heiderose, and Andreas Fischer-Nagel. *A Look Through the Mousehole*. The Carolrhoda Nature Watch Book Series. Minneapolis, Minn.: Carolrhoda, 1989.

Peer through the eyes of a camera into the tiny world of mice, living in barns and houses as they raise their young, search for food, and try to avoid the sharp claws of a resident cat. Excellent color photographs highlight the series.

Lewison, Wendy Chayette. *Going to Sleep on the Farm*. Illustrated by Jan Wÿngaard. New York: Dial Books Young, 1992.

Quiet jewel of a book gives a glimpse of farm animals that go to sleep on the farm. Especially for the very young child.

McFarland, Cynthia. *Cows in the Parlor: A Visit to a Dairy Farm*. New York: Atheneum, 1990.

A typical day on a dairy farm is the subject of this photo essay. Children will find out how a milking machine works, as well as what a cow and her calves eat. Young children will gain an understanding of how milk gets from the cow to the cup.

Paladino, Catherine. *Our Vanishing Farm* Animals. Boston: Little, Brown, 1991.

An interesting examination of the new breed of animals in danger of becoming extinct—the farm animals—including the Dutch belted cow, Guinea hog, and American Bashkir curly horse. Will be especially intriguing for the older reader, but the younger child will delight in the rich, color photographs.

Animals: Insects

Aylesworth, Jim. *Old Black Fly*. Illustrated by Stephen Gammell. New York: Henry Holt, 1992.

Illustrates how a mischievous old black fly buzzes through the alphabet, in rhymed text. Children sing the text to the tune of "Shoo-Fly." Jim teaches first grade in Oak Park, Illinois.

Carle, Eric. *The Grouchy Ladybug.* New York: Harper & Row, 1977.

Carle uses pages in odd sizes to show the passage of time and the growth of the ladybug's adversaries.

Other highly recommended books by Carle are *The Honeybee and The Robber, The Very Busy Spider, The Very Quiet Cricket,* and *The Very Hungry Caterpillar.*

Fischer-Nagel, Heiderose, and Andreas Fischer-Nagel. *An Ant Colony/The Housefly.* Carolrhoda Nature Watch Book Series. Minneapolis, Minn.: Carolrhoda, 1989.

Excellent color photographs distinguish this well-thought-out series. An Ant Colony takes a look at the life cycle and daily routine of ants, as well as the amazing tasks ants can accomplish.

Most people think of flies as pests, but in ancient Egypt a fly was a symbol of bravery. Best of all, these common household insects are trash eaters, breaking down manure and dead matter into nearly odorless materials that enrich the soil. Read The Housefly and find out more.

Fleming, Denise. *In the Tall, Tall Grass.* New York: Henry Holt, 1991.

Rhymed text (crunch, munch, caterpillar's lunch) presents a toddler's view of creatures found in the grass from lunchtime until nightfall, such as bees, ants, and moles.

Florian, Douglas. *Discovering Butterflies.* New York: Aladdin, 1986.

Describes structure, life cycle, and behavior of butterflies and depicts different species found in North America, Africa, and South America. Questions like "How are butterflies hatched?" "Where do they go when it's cold?" or "How many kinds of butterflies are there?" are clearly explained through text and colorful illustrations.

Fowler, Allan. *It's A Good Thing There Are Insects.* Chicago: Children's Press, 1990.

These realistic pictures identify the characteristics of insects and describe some of their useful activities and products.

Gibbons, Gail. *Monarch Butterfly.* New York: Holiday House, 1989.

Describes the life cycle, body parts, and behavior of the monarch butterfly. Includes instructions on how to raise the monarch.

Jeunesse, Gallimard, and Pascale de Bourgoing. *The Ladybug and Other Insects.* Illustrated by Sylvie Perols. Cartwheel Book Series. New York: Scholastic, 1991.

This is one in a series of spectacular books that allow young children to watch a ladybug lay eggs on a leaf, see larvae turn into mature insects, and more . . .

Other books in the series include *Colors, Fruit, The Tree, Weather,* and *The Egg.*

Pallotta, Jerry. *The Icky Bug Counting Book.* Illustrated by Masiello. Mass.: Charlesbridge Pub., 1992.

This clever book catches children's imagination and also provides countless tidbits of information on bugs.

Parker, John. *I Love Spiders.* Illustrated by Rita Parkinson. New York: Ashton Scholastic, 1988.

A wonderful introduction to spiders and their world, written especially for the emergent reader.

Parker, Nancy Winslow. *Bugs.* Cartwheel Book Series. New York: Mulberry Books, 1987.

"What slippery bug made Doug say 'ugh'? A Slug." Slugs, spiders, centipedes, and other creepy creatures can be found in this delightful encyclopedia of insects for young readers combining funny rhymes, scientific drawings, and solid facts. Bugs is a pleasant introduction to 16 familiar animals.

Patent, Dorothy. *Looking at Ants.* New York: Holiday House, 1989.

A close look at the fascinating world of ants through the eyes of the camera lens. Effective black and white photos complement the intriguing text.

Schnieper, Claudia. *Amazing Spiders.* Photographs by Max Meier. Carolrhoda Nature Watch Book Series. Minneapolis, Minn.: Carolrhoda, 1989.

With intriguing close-ups of varieties of spiders, the well-written text introduces the reader to some of the 30,000 known species found in gardens, fields, and houses. Outstanding color photographs focus on fascinating details of spider life.

Souza, D.M. *Eight Legs/Insects in the Garden/Insects Around the House/What Bit Me?.* Creatures All Around Us Series. Minneapolis, Minn.: Carolrhoda, 1991.

Eight Legs describes life cycles of various spiders and other arachnids, including the crab spider, wolf spider, and whipscorpion, with clear, close-up color photographs.

Insects in the Garden invites the reader to take a look around and meet many insects at work. They can be as tiny as a beetle, small enough to fit through an eye of a needle, or as big as a stick insect—over a foot long!

Out of billions of insects living on the earth today, hundreds may be crawling around outside your house. A few may be inside, tasting carpets, books, sweaters, and even your socks. Insects Around the House takes a look at a few of them, their habits, and their unusual appetites.

Ants, mosquitoes, and waterbugs are some common insects that feast on warm bodies—dogs, cats, and even you. What Bit Me? takes a close look at such insects as head lice.

Suzuki, David. *Looking At Insects.* Teacher's Guide. New York: Wiley, 1992.

Did you know that insects have been around 300 times as long as people and that there are as many different kinds of beetles as there are plants in the world? Amazing facts, projects, and scientific investigations fill this fun and knowledgeable guide to insects. Clear, detailed activities like building beetle traps, making clover syrup, and starting an ant village can be easily followed by young children. The best teacher resource I know.

What's Inside? Insects. A first guide to the wonders and workings of insects. New York: Dorling Kindersley, 1992.

Illustrates what's inside a chrysalis as well as why a fly is able to walk on the ceiling.

Wood, Audrey. *Quick As a Cricket.* Illustrated by Don Wood. Chicago: Child's Play, 1982.

"I'm as quick as a cricket, slow as a snail, small as an ant, large as a whale . . . put it all together, you've got Me!" Excellent drawings of a variety of animals for very young children.

Animals: Pets

Arnold, Caroline. *A Guide Dog Puppy Grows Up.* Photographs by
    Richard Hewett. New York: Harcourt Brace Jovanovich, 1991.

Following the career of a guide dog, this informative book
focuses on the first year of life for this puppy, including her
training and ultimate placement with a blind person.
Encourages empathy for both animals and the blind.

Evans, Mark. *ASPCA Pet Care Guides for Kids.* New York:
    Dorling Kindersley, 1992.

Practical guides for caring for pets—guinea pigs, rabbits,
kittens, and puppies. A "must" series for any pet, includes a pet
fact sheet and what to do if you go on vacation. A welcomed
new series to classroom pets.

McMillan, Bruce. *Kitten Can. . . .* New York: Lothrop, 1984.

A photographic essay focusing on a playful kitten during a
day's romp. Truly memorable photographs, carefully selected,
complement a beginner's text.

Pets: An Eye Openers Book. Photographs by Michael Dunning.
    New York: Aladdin, 1991.

A member of this stunningly designed series for the very
youngest child. This book offers a few simple facts about each
pet on each page that surrounds a vibrant, life-like photograph
of each animal. Similar to the Eyewitness Juniors series, but
aimed at a younger age.

Animals: Reptiles

Clarke, Barry. *Amazing Frogs and Toads.* Photographed by Jerry
    Young. The Eyewitness Juniors Book Series. New York:
    Knopf, 1990.

A close-up look at some of the world's most amazing frogs
and toads done in the incredible Eyewitness format. Even the

borders depict various species of frogs so life-like they almost jump off the page.

A miniature version of the Eyewitness series that is published for the older child.

Gross, Ruth B. *Snakes*. New York: Four Winds, 1990.

Examines a few of the thousands of different kinds of snakes in the world. A special section of color photographs is devoted to 19 of the most interesting snakes in the United States and Canada, including four poisonous ones.

Kuchalla, Susan. *What Is a Reptile?*. Illustrated by Paul Harvey. The Now I Know Series. Mahwah, N.J.: Troll Associates, 1982.

A wonderful guide for the beginning reader, with colorful illustrations throughout and sparse text.

Lauber, Patricia. *Snakes Are Hunters*. Illustrated by Holly Keller. Let's Read and Find Out Series. New York: Harper, 1988.

A beginning guide to snakes, describing their behavior, eating habits, and life cycle. Developmentally appropriate and interesting for young children. There are over 100 books in this special series.

Mazer, Anne. *The Salamander Room*. Illustrated by Steve Johnson. New York: Knopf, 1991.

A young boy discovers a salamander in the woods and quietly dreams about building the perfect home for his new-found companion.

Pringle, Laurence. Batman: *Exploring the World of Bats*. Photographs by Merlin Tuttle. New York: Scribner's, 1991.

An informative and intriguing look at bats in their natural habitats for the older reader. Describes scientist Merlin Tuttle's research and uses his stunning photographs.

Schnieper, Claudia. *Chameleons/Lizards*. Photographs by Max Meier. Carolrhoda Nature Watch Book Series. Minneapolis, Minn.: Carolrhoda, 1989, 1990.

Chameleons pictures these creatures of every size, shape, and species in vivid detail. A glossary in the back helps explain scientific vocabulary like pigments or melanin.

Did you know that some kinds of lizards don't have legs and that others can taste the air? Do you know why lizards change color or why they bask in the sun? *Lizards* has answers to all these questions and more. You'll be amazed by the variety of lizards in this Nature Watch book, which covers lizards from the Arctic to Southern Italy. Outstanding color photographs.

Tarrant, Graham. *Frogs*. Illustrated by Tony King. New York: Putnam, 1983.

A well designed pop-up book about frogs in participation format. A memorable read-aloud about the life cycle of a frog. Not to be missed!

Animals: Wildlife

Ashby, Ruth. *Jane Goodall's Animal World: Tigers*. New York: Atheneum, 1990.

Under the leadership of the world's foremost naturalist Jane Goodall, this engaging series with full color photographs focuses on environment, family relationships, and ecological positions of tigers. Especially geared for independent readers.

Bantock, Nick. *Runners, Sliders, Bouncers, Climbers: A Pop-Up Look at Animals in Motion*. New York: Hyperion, 1992.

An action-packed, fun- and fact-filled book that shows young children ways in which animals and humans move.

Emberley, Rebecca. *Jungle Sounds*. Boston: Little, Brown, 1989.

Toucans, mandrills, ants, and gibbons are some of the jungle creatures that you will hear in this book, which is illustrated with striking paper cutouts.

Larsen, Thor. *The Polar Bear Family Book*. Needham, Mass.: Picture Book Studio, 1990.

The life of a polar bear family is depicted against the backdrop of an Arctic scene, illustrated with stunning color photographs by leading marine biologist Thor Larsen. Newborn cubs are seen exploring their environment using their instincts and intelligence to survive in their surroundings.

Morozumi, Atsuko. *One Gorilla*. New York: Farrar, 1990.

This New York Times Best Illustrated Book depicts many animals in a simple counting book format with delicate humor. These illustrations are not to be missed.

Parsons, Alexandra. *Amazing Cats*. Photographs by Jerry Young. The Eyewitness Juniors Book Series. New York: Knopf, 1990.

A close-up look at why leopards have spots and how cats see in the dark, along with other fascinating facts that children will devour. Amazing stories, such as the tale of the pet cat from Turkey that loves to swim or Androcles and the lion, will highlight curiosity.

Pferrer, Pierre. *Bears, Big and Little*. Young Discovery Library Series. Ossining, N.Y.: 1989.

What does a grizzly bear eat? Why do polar bears travel? How does a mother bear raise her young? These are some of the questions answered in this wonderful series of discovery books for young children, containing over 120 titles.

Russell, William. *Animal Families of the Wild*. Illustrated by John Butler. New York: Crown, 1990.

An anthology of works about animal families of the wild from some of the best-known writers of our time, including James Michener and Roger Caras. Each story is suitable to be read aloud to children and is prefaced by a thoughtful introduction that provides viewpoints on animal behavior. This book will add much to the growing awareness of environmental and wildlife issues.

Schlein, Miriam. *Jane Goodall's Animal World: Pandas*. New York: Aladdin, 1989.

Introduces the life cycle, behavior, and characteristics of these much admired creatures, with accurate notes from the famous naturalist Jane Goodall.

Simon, Seymour. *Big Cats*. New York: Harper Collins, 1991.

Some kind of big cat is found on every continent of the world except Europe, Australia, and Antarctica, yet many are close to extinction because land is taken from the wild for farming and human habitation. This clear, simple text with stunning full color photographs shows how the lion, tiger, leopard, jaguar, puma, cheetah, and snow leopard enrich our world.

Animals: Zoo

Brennan, John, and Leonie Keaney. *Zoo Day*. Minneapolis, Minn.: Carolrhoda, 1989.

Hour-by-hour description of a typical day in the zoo, including the feeding of various animals, with interesting color photographs.

Florian, Douglas. *At the Zoo*. New York: Greenwillow, 1992.

In his unique, simple style, Douglas Florian portrays animals at the zoo with labeled drawings that appeal to the young child. Other books by author-artist Florian include *A Winter Day, A Summer Day, A Year in the Country, A Beach Day*, and *Nature Watch*.

McMillan, Bruce. *The Baby Zoo*. New York: Scholastic, 1992.

Baby zoo animals photographed at the San Diego and St. Louis zoos are clearly photo-illustrated. Maps indicating where each animal comes from are included.

Zoo Animals: An Eye Openers Book. Photographs by Philip Dowell. New York: Aladdin, 1991.

Zoo animals are the subject of this book in the well designed and brilliantly visual series. Specific body parts are highlighted with individual illustrations that surround the main photographs. Each animal comes alive when you turn each page. Could be used as a display poster.

Astronomy

Cole, JoAnna. *The Magic School Bus Lost in the Solar System*. Illustrated by Bruce Degen. New York: Scholastic, 1990.

A journey to outer space is in store for the children in Mrs. Frizzle's class as they travel through the solar system and learn about the planets and other scientific facts about space, including why Mars is red and why it doesn't rain on Venus.

Gallant, Roy A. *The Constellations*. New York: Four Winds, 1991.

This guide to identifying the constellations serves as an excellent teacher's resource. An explanation of the mythology surrounding constellations is interesting and informative.

Lauber, Patricia. *Journey to the Planets.* New York: Crown, 1990.

This revised edition, using new photos and information collected by the Voyager explorations, incorporates stunning black and white photography and clear, well-written text to highlight the prominent features of each planet in our solar system.

Birds

Amazing Birds. Eyewitness Juniors Series. New York: Alfred Knopf, 1990.

A close-up look at the world's amazing birds and some intriguing questions—How does a hummingbird hum? Why are flamingos pink? This series, on almost every topic, is not to be missed.

Arnold, Caroline. *Saving the Peregrine Falcon.* Photographs by Richard Hewett. Minneapolis, Minn.: Carolrhoda, 1985.

A 1985 School Library Journal Best Book for Children. Clear, detailed pictures intertwined with text examine the plight of the peregrine falcon and current efforts to save them from extinction. As part of the campaign to increase their population, conservationists are also releasing the falcons in cities and encouraging them to nest on top of tall buildings, cathedrals, and bridges.

Bailey, Donna. *Facts About: Birds.* The Facts About Series. Madison, N.J.: Steck-Vaughn, 1990.

Answers questions many young children will ask about birds with detailed illustrations and photographs. Topics include different types of birds, how birds fly, birds in different habitats, and nests and eggs. An excellent introduction to our feathered friends.

Other titles in the series include *Fish, Reptiles, Insects,* and *Space.*

Bailey, Donna, and David Burnie. *Birds.* Eyewitness Explorers Series. New York: Dorling Kindersley, 1992.

In an innovative visual layout, birds are presented in their many habitats—woodlands, the tropics, cities. A lively book for your display science table.

Bash, Barbara. *Urban Roosts.* Sierra Club Book Series. Boston: Little, Brown, 1990.

Describes various birds that make their homes in the heart of the city, including barn owls, night hawks, and falcons. Brilliant, realistic, watercolor illustrations reflect the true splendor of city life as birds find creative nesting places in curved storefront letters, old shoes, or work gloves. A fascinating book examining the adaptability and resilience of urban wildlife.

Other books in the series are *Desert Giant* and *Tree of Life.*

Buckley, Virginia. *State Birds.* Illustrated by Arthur and Alan Singer. New York: Lodestar/Dutton, 1986.

Detailed portrayal of the birds representing each of our 50 states, from the rare Hawaiian goose to the colorful purple finch of New Hampshire, shown in typical habitats. Informative text highlights origins, characteristics and significance. Also includes dates and reasons for each state's selection. Designed by world famous bird artists.

Butterworth, Christine. *Eagles.* Animal World Series. National Education Corp, 1990.

A first reading text about eagles, with photographs, illustrations, and general facts describing characteristics and habits.

Other titles in the series include *Kangaroos, Bears, Frogs,* and *Snakes.*

Dewey, Jennifer. *Birds of Antarctica.* Boston: Little, Brown, 1989.

A well researched book takes the reader through a year in the life of a penguin. Exquisite, detailed drawings illustrate all aspects of a penguin's life and behavior, set against the dramatic background of Antarctica. Will expand and nurture ideas in Mr. Popper's Penguins.

Ehlert, Lois. *Feathers for Lunch.* New York: Harcourt Brace Jovanovich, 1990.

Following a hungry cat on his quest for lunch, the young reader encounters 12 common birds and a glossary of facts—a lot more than what the cat gets! The bright, life-size portraits of each bird and engaging story will intrigue both children and adults.

Flora. *Feathers Like a Rainbow.* New York: Harper & Row, 1989.

An exotic folk tale about birds of the Amazon rain forest, including the macaw, toucan, and ibis. Based on the legend of the hummingbird.

Holder, Heidi. *Crows.* New York: Farrar, 1987.

More than a counting book for young children, this text is based on historical research on the superstitions around crows and magpies. The design of the lettering and exquisite illustrations enhance the historical flavor.

Lang, Aubrey. *Eagles.* Photographs by Wayne Lynch. Boston: Little, Brown, 1990.

Did you know that when two eaglets are waiting for dinner, the bigger one will always be fed first? This is one of the many interesting facts that are presented in this richly photographed volume about the king of birds. Includes environmental concerns about the future of eagles.

Oppenheim, Joanne. *Have You Seen Birds?* Pictures by Barbara Reid. New York: Scholastic, 1986.

Vibrant, elegant, textured illustrations describe different types of birds for young children in rhymed text. Colorful plasticine is creatively used to form the detailed renderings. Also produced as a big book.

Parsons, Alexandra. *Amazing Birds.* Photographs by Jerry Young. Eyewitness Juniors Series. New York: Knopf, 1990.

A first guide to intriguing birds such as the ostrich, peacock, and flamingo, with a unique combination of illustrations and photographs. The unusual design of this whole series centers around a large, close-up photograph on each page intertwined with sketches and fascinating details that encourage curiosity. The kind of book that should be in every waiting room where kids will be tempted to pick it up.

Peterson, Roger. *Peterson First Guide to Birds.* Boston: Houghton, Mifflin, 1986.

An abridged version of the famous Peterson Field Guides, this pocket version is perfect for field trips and will help children get started identifying birds.

Pomerantz, Charlotte. *Flap Your Wings and Try.* Illustrated by Nancy Tafuri. New York: Greenwillow, 1989.

In typical Tafuri style, youngest children will delight in the picture storybook about a young bird trying to fly. Perfect story for a child beginning to read on his or her own.

Schindler, S.D. *My First Bird Book.* New York: Random House, 1989.

An easy-to-assemble mobile highlights this excellent first look at birds in different habitats and answers the question "What makes a bird a bird?" Richly detailed illustrations make bird watching easier and present creative ideas for constructing bird feeders.

Schlein, Miriam. *Pigeons.* Photographs by Margaret Miller. New York: Crowell, 1989.

Engaging anecdotes and a stunning photo essay portray the life and habits of pigeons and their city families. Effective black and white photographs depict famous pigeons who have rescued people at sea and been messengers for spies. An intimate look at the unusual life of the common city bird.

Tejima. *Owl Lake.* New York: Philomel, 1982.

Stunning, bold, woodcut illustrations charm young readers as they follow Father Owl on his quest to feed his family. A treasured story, which evokes timeless feelings about nature's night creatures and depicts the beauty of Hokkaido, Japan's northern-most island. A work of art.

Tejima. *Swan Sky.* New York, Philomel, 1988.

A poignant story about the migration of swans and the cycle of life and death. The elegant woodcuttings resonate with the beauty and grace of swans.

Usborne Spotter's Guides. *Birds of North America* by Dr. Philip Burton. Tulsa, Okla.: EDC, 1991.

A pocketbook guide that helps you identify over 170 species of birds and lets you check them off.

Colors

Ardley, Neil. *The Science Book of Color.* New York: Harcourt Brace Jovanovich, 1991.

The scientific principles of color are explained through clear photographs and simple yet interesting projects. Make a rainbow appear on a piece of white paper or write a secret message in invisible ink.

Other titles in the series include *Air*, *Light*, and *Water*.

Bailey, Vanessa. *Animal Colors*. New York: Barron, 1991.

Explores colors using parts of animals' bodies. Large, lively illustrations and a story.

Kirkpatrick, Rena K. *Rainbow Colors*. Illustrated by Anna Barnard. Milwaukee: Macdonald-Raintree, 1985.

Explains how a rainbow is formed and suggests activities to explore this concept (e.g., using soap bubbles, a fish tank, prisms). Also explores colors found in nature.

McMillan, Bruce. *Growing Colors*. New York: Lothrop.

Bruce McMillan's typically stunning color photographs create another masterpiece with photos of green peas, yellow corn, purple plums, and other fruits and vegetables that brilliantly display the colors of nature. For the youngest reader.

York, Jane, ed. *My First Look at Colors*. New York: Random House, 1990.

Photographs of familiar objects introduce colors to young children. A well-designed book.

Dinosaurs

Barton, Byron. *Bones, Bones, Dinosaur Bones*. New York: Crowell, 1990.

In typical bold, bright, exuberant pictures, Byron Barton writes a story about six paleontologists who search for dinosaur bones. The rhythmic text almost sings and is perfect for the youngest child.

Eyewitness Books. *Dinosaur.* New York: Knopf, 1991.

This series continues to set new standards for excellence in non-fiction, with its informative content and photographic displays.

Other titles include: *Fish, Fossils, Horse, Film, Boat, Mammal, Insect,* and *Plant.*

Gay, Tanner Ottley. *Dinosaurs in Action.* Illustrated by Jean Cassels. New York: Aladdin, 1990.

The world of dinosaurs comes to life through a well-designed pop-up book that features nine of the most well known of the ancient creatures. A world map illustrates the location of many dinosaur fossils.

Lauber, Patricia. *Living With Dinosaurs.* Illustrated by Douglas Henderson. New York: Bradbury, 1991.

In a realistically illustrated book, award-winning author Patricia Lauber gives the reader a sight-and sound-filled tour of the vanished world of 75 million years ago in prehistoric Montana, which had a seashore. Includes a section on how a fossil forms and later comes to life.

Schlein, Miriam. *Discovering Dinosaur Babies.* Illustrated by Margaret Colbert. New York: Four Winds, 1991.

This intriguing text traces clues left by 12 different dinosaurs and their young. Through fossilized eggs, nests, teeth, and bones, the reader discovers how prehistoric animals cared for their young.

Thompson, C.E. *Dinosaur Bones!* Illustrated by Paige Billin-Frye. New York: Putnam, 1992.

A very fine first text that includes the makings of a mobile from which to hang all seven dinosaurs. One side of each dinosaur includes an exterior illustration and the other side has a glow-in-the-dark skeleton!

West, Robin. *Dinosaur Discoveries*. Photographs by Bob and Diane Wolfe. Minneapolis, Minn.: Carolrhoda, 1989.

Instructions for drawing, cutting, and gluing paper shapes together to form three-dimensional paper dinosaurs. Well-detailed directions with colored photographs of the finished product.

Ecology

Arnold, Caroline. *A Walk Up the Mountain/A Walk in the Desert*. Illustrated by Freya Tanz. First Facts Series. Eden Prairie, Minn.: Silver, 1990.

A beginning series for the youngest reader. In A Walk Up the Mountain, one encounters an eagle, a pika, and even mountain goats. A lively glossary features mountains around the world and a few creatures you might find along the route.

A hungry hawk, cactus, and the poisonous Gila monster are among the things one meets in A Walk in the Desert. A colorful map reviews adventures along each route.

Other titles in the series include *A Walk by the Seashore* and *A Walk in the Woods*.

Cole, JoAnna. *The Magic School Bus Inside the Earth*. Illustrated by Bruce Degen. New York: Scholastic, 1987.

Join Ms. Frizzle and her class as they journey deep inside the earth and discover different layers and learn how they were formed, and then return with a fabulous rock collection for their classroom. A fun-filled and humorous experience focusing on helpful scientific facts.

Dewey, Jennifer Owings. *A Night and Day in the Desert.* Boston: Little, Brown, 1991.

Stunning full-page illustrations and informative text depict the unique environment of the desert, complete with a howling coyote, prickly cactus, hot days, and cool nights.

Dorros, Arthur. *Rain Forest Secrets.* New York: Scholastic, 1990.

Bright illustrations and simple, informative text describe the characteristics of the rain forest ecosystem. Encounter gorillas, anteaters, and other animals and plants that live in the rain forest environment. Includes a brief discussion of the destruction of the rain forests.

Gelman, Rita. *Dawn to Dusk in the Galapagos.* Photographs by Tui De Roy. Boston: Little Brown, 1991.

The rare beauty of the Galapagos islands can be discovered through this engaging display of amazing photographs and well-written text. Meet a vast array of unique creatures, including the blue-footed booby and the albatross.

George, Jean Craighead. *Who Really Killed Cock Robin?* New York: Harper, 1991.

A dedicated and concerned eighth grader encounters baffling facts and environmental evidence in solving the ecological mystery of what imbalances really killed the town's famous robin. For the older reader.

George, Jean Craighead. *One Day in the Woods.* Illustrated by Gary Allen. New York: Crowell, 1988.

The beauty and ecology of the Northeastern Deciduous Forest is explored through thoughtful text and exquisite black and white drawings, as a young girl journeys through the forest on a search for the ovenbird.

Gibbons, Gail. *Recycle.* Boston: Little, Brown, 1992.

Large, legible type and clear illustrations invite readers in and explain the recycling process from start to finish and what happens to paper, plastic, and other recyclable items.

Lauber, Patricia. *How We Learned the Earth Is Round.* Illustrated by Megan Lloyd. New York: Crowell, 1990.

Bright illustrations and engaging text explain various changes in beliefs about the shape of the earth, including the flat earth theories, until the voyages of Columbus and Magellan proved that the earth was indeed round.

Lowery, Linda. *Earth Day.* Illustrated by Mary Bergherr. Minneapolis, Minn.: Carolrhoda, 1991.

From the first Earth Day in 1970, to the annual celebrations that started in 1990, this book reflects upon the importance of environmental awareness and concern of people of all ages. It also describes special activities planned to solve the problems of pollution, waste, and destruction of our earth.

Suzuki, David. *Looking At the Environment.* With Barbara Hehner. The Looking At . . . Series. New York: Wiley, 1992.

An introduction to amazing facts and educational projects concerning our environment. Readers learn that over 90% of the world's animals are insects and that the earth uses the same water over and over. Learn to test your air for pollution and make your own solar panel.

Usborne Starting Points in Science Series. *Where Does Rubbish Go?* Tulsa, Okla.: EDC, 1992.

A new, exciting series for young children explains how rubbish can be recycled. Gives an intriguing historical view through a picture format.

Growing Things

Bjork, Christina. *Linnea's Windowsill* Garden. Illustrated by Lena Anderson. New York: R&S Books, 1988.

Linnea expresses her love of plants by keeping this journal of exciting and interesting activities and facts about various types of flowers and greenery. Learn to make garden-cress cheese, plant and grow an orange tree, and the art of watering.

Black, Irma Simonton. *Busy Seeds.* Illustrated by Robert Quackenbush. New York: Holiday House, 1970.

This imaginative introduction to the world of growing things explains very simply how trees, vines, flowers, and leaves grow from seeds.

Brice, Raphaelle. *Rice—The Little Grain that Feeds the World.* Illustrated by Aline Riquier. Ossining, New York: Young Discovery Library, 1984.

Translated from the French, these tiny books hold capsule information on a multitude of topics—an encyclopedia you can keep in your pocket. There are 120 titles in the series.

Carlstrom, Nancy White. *Moose in the Garden.* Illustrated by Lisa Desimini. New York: Harper, 1990.

Simple, rhythmic verse and vibrant paintings detail the growth of a family's garden until a very hungry moose decides to visit. For the youngest reader.

Other books by the author include *Wild, Wild Sunflower Child Anna.*

Cooney, Barbara. *Miss Rumphius.* New York: Puffin, 1982.

To make the world beautiful, Miss Rumphius plants flowers (lupines) everywhere.

Cork, Barbara. *Mysteries and Marvels of Plant Life.* Illustrated by Ian Jackson. Tulsa, Okla.: EDC, 1983.

Facts and pictures of plants and plant life pack the pages of this informative guide. A helpful index organizes the information, while intriguing true/false questions are answered at the back of the book.

Ehlert, Lois. *Planting a Rainbow.* New York: Harcourt Brace Jovanovich, 1988.

In another masterpiece, Lois Ehlert's brilliant pictures detail the planting of bulbs, seeds, and plants as they sprout into a rainbow of colorful blossoms.

Other books by Ehlert include *Eating the Alphabet, Feathers for Lunch,* and *Red Leaf, Yellow Leaf.*

Fife, Dale H. *The Empty Lot.* Illustrated by Jim Arnosky. Boston: Little, Brown, 1991.

A touching story of a man who discovers that his once empty lot is now full of life. That lot is now home to plants, animals, and insects. Reflects on the importance of the symbiotic relationship between man and nature.

Gibbons, Gail. *The Seasons of Arnold's Apple Tree.* New York: A Voyager/HBJ Book, Harcourt Brace Jovanovich, 1992.

Arnold enjoys the apple tree as the seasons pass. Includes a recipe for apple pie and a description of a cider press.

————. *From Seed to Plant.* New York: Holiday House, 1991.

Gibbons' bright and active illustrations and well-written text explore the intricate relationship between seeds and the plants that they produce.

Heller, Ruth. *The Reason for a Flower.* New York: Grosset, 1983.

This beautifully illustrated book eloquently teaches some of the basics of botany to children in an interesting way. Some concepts taught are pollination and the interdependency of plants and animals.

Other books by Heller include *Flowers That Never Bloom* and *Chickens Aren't the Only Ones.*

Jennings, Terry. *SEEDS.* Junior Science Series. Illustrated by David Anstey. New York: Gloucester Press, 1990.

Clear illustrations and simple text introduce children to activities and experiments.

Jordan, Helena. *How a Seed Grows.* Illustrated by Loretta Krupinski. New York: HarperCollins, 1992.

A bean seed is planted in an eggshell and lots of other seeds also begin to grow. A great multicultural book.

Kellogg, Cynthia. *Corn: What It Is, What It Does.* Illustrated by Tom Huffman. New York: Greenwillow, 1989.

An interesting introduction to corn and its many uses in the home, at school, and in industry.

Lauber, Patricia. *From Flower to Flower: Animals and Pollination/Seeds: Pop, Stick, Glide.* Photographs by Jerome Wexler. New York: Crown, 1986, 1981.

In *From Flower to Flower*, revealing black and white photographs and informative text examine the role of animals in the pollination process. Stunning black and white photographs and well-written text are also featured in Seeds, which examines the many different ways flowering plants disperse their seeds.

Lobel, Anita. *Allison's Zinnia.* New York: Greenwillow, 1990.

"Allison acquired an Amaryllis for Beryl, Beryl bought a Begonia for Crystal . . ." and so on through the alphabet. The strikingly realistic painting of each flower creates a beautiful garden that doesn't require water.

Mayes, Susan. *What Makes a Flower Grow?*. Illustrated by Brin Edwards and Mike Pringle. Tulsa, Okla.: EDC, 1989.

A beginning guide to plant life, growth, and pollination. Simple text and clear color drawings enhance the learning experience.

Other titles in the series are *Prehistoric Animals* and *A World After Dinosaurs.*

McMillan, Bruce. *Growing Colors.* New York: Lothrop.

Bruce McMillan's typically stunning color photographs create another masterpiece of photos of green peas, yellow corn, purple plums, and other fruits and vegetables that brilliantly display the colors of nature.

Patent, Dorothy Henshaw. *Where Food Comes From.* Photographs by William Munoz. New York: Holiday House, 1991.

Did you know that yogurt is alive? That carrots and radishes are roots? These are two interesting facts that are explained through clear text and bright color photographs detailing how grains, dairy, meats, vegetables, and fruits become our food.

Rogow, Zack. *Oranges.* Illustrated by Mary Szilagyi. New York: Orchard, 1988.

Clear text and colorful illustrations describe the long journey and the combined labor of the many people it takes to produce a single orange from tree to table.

Sanchez, Isidro, and Peris, Carme. *The Garden*. New York: Barron, 1991.

Words and pictures introduce children to plant life in the garden. A helpful section at the end of the book helps parents and teachers answer questions that children might ask.

Other books in the series are *The Forest, The Farm, The Orchard, The Seasons,* and *The Five Senses*.

Thompson, Ruth. *Trees*. Usborne First Nature Series. Tulsa, Okla.: EDC, 1990.

Busy, competent introductory book on this nature topic.

Titherington, Jeanne. *Pumpkin, Pumpkin*. New York: Scholastic, 1986.

Exquisite, textured illustrations detail the birth and life of a pumpkin from spring planting to fall picking. Perfect for the youngest reader.

Wexler, Jerome. *Flowers, Fruits, Seeds*. New York: Simon & Schuster, 1987.

Clear photographs of various plants and trees show characteristics of different leaves, seeds, and flowers. Includes coconut seeds, seeds that are rough, small seeds, and even poisonous seeds.

The Human Body

Aliki. *My Feet*. New York: Crowell, 1990.

Walking, running, skipping, marching, and kicking are just a few of the activities we can do with our feet. Aliki's bright illustrations and simple text focus on another important part of the human body.

Aliki. *My Hands.* New York: Crowell, 1990.

Simple text and vivid, active illustrations describe our hands and the many ways they are important to us. For the youngest reader.

Cole, JoAnna. *The Magic School Bus Inside the Human Body.* Illustrated by Bruce Degen. New York: Scholastic, 1989.

Another class field trip takes Ms. Frizzle and her students inside the human body to explore first-hand the parts of the body and how they work. Filled with interesting and informative facts.

Dorling Kindersley. *The Body and How It Works.* Boston: Houghton Mifflin, 1992.

Part of the See & Explore Library, this book is just one in another superb series.
Other titles include *Birds and How They Live* and *Animals and Where They Live.*

Evans, David, and Claudette Williams. *Me and My Body.* New York: Dorling Kindersley, 1992.

Clear action photographs encourage children to investigate and to use their senses to find out about science. Concentrates on the structure of the body, senses, and also diet. Part of the unique Let's Explore Science Series. Other titles in this new series: *Make It Balance, Make It Change, Make It Go.*

Markle, Sandra. *Outside and Inside You.* New York: Bradbury, 1991.

Full-color photographs illustrate the various parts of the human body and their functions. See a tooth developing under the gums and view your muscles through a microscope. A helpful glossary summarizes each body part.

Suzuki, David. *Looking At The Body*. With Barbara Hehner. The
Looking At . . . Series. New York: Wiley, 1992.

Did you know that a baby has more bones than an adult?
Discover this and other amazing facts about the human body
along with fun activities and projects. Listen to your own
heartbeat or measure how big a breath you can take.

"Light"en Up

Ardley, Neil. *The Science Book of Light*. New York: Harcourt
Brace Jovanovich, 1991.

Several interesting and illuminating experiments
demonstrate the principles of light. Full color photographs give
step-by-step instructions for each experiment.
Other titles in the series include *Air, Color,* and *Water*.

Berger, Melvin. *Switch On, Switch Off*. Illustrated by Carolyn
Cross. New York: Harper, 1989.

Active drawings and clear text explain how electricity is
produced and transmitted and even tells how to create
electricity using a wire and a magnet.

Webb, Angela. *Talk about Reflections*. Photography by Chris
Fairclough. London: Franklin Watts, 1988.

Colorful photos and simple text explain how light affects
everyday things, particularly through reflections. Suggests
simple activities.

The Ocean and Its Creatures

Arnold, Caroline. *A Walk By the Seashore*. Illustrated by Freya
Tanz. The First Facts Series. Eden Prairie, Minn.: Silver,
1990.

A beginning series for the youngest reader focuses on a walk by the seashore, where a child can observe plants, animals, sand, and the waves. A lively glossary and a colorful map review adventures along each route.

Other books in the series include *A Walk in the Desert, A Walk Up the Mountains,* and *A Walk in the Woods.*

Cossi, Olga. *Harp Seals.* Minneapolis, Minn.: Carolrhoda, 1991.

Through exquisite, close-up photographs of these amazing sea creatures, the reader is introduced to the life cycle of the harp seals who live in the freezing waters of the Arctic Circle.

Gay, Tanner O. *Sharks in Action.* Illustrated by Jean Cassels. New York: Aladdin, 1990.

How do sharks swim? Do they ever lose their teeth? Do mother sharks take care of their baby pups? These are some of the questions answered in this well designed, pop-up action book for the youngest reader.

Gelman, Rita Golden. *Monsters of the Sea.* Illustrated by Jean Day Zallinger. Boston: Little, Brown, 1990.

Brief text and full-page illustrations depict 12 giant sea creatures, some prehistoric and some modern.

Gibbons, Gail. *Surrounded by Sea.* Boston: Little, Brown, 1991.

A seasonal exploration of the activities and environment of a contemporary small New England fishing village.

Gunzi, Christiane. *Tide Pool.* Look Closer Series. New York: Dorling Kindersley, 1992.

Another series that is marvelous! This book is a whole unit of study. With clear photographs, life in a tide pool comes alive.

Heller, Ruth. *How to Hide an Octopus & Other Sea Creatures.* New York: Grosset, 1985.

A small book filled with wonder that tells, in Ruth Heller's typical clever, careful way, how creatures are camouflaged.

Lauber, Patricia. *An Octopus Is Amazing.* Illustrated by Holly Keller. New York: Crowell, 1990.

Did you know that a clever octopus can take off the top of a glass jar to get a crab inside? In this book, the reader gets to know the amazing life of the octopus.

Lazier, Christine. *Seashore Life.* Illustrated by Graham Underhill. The Young Discovery Library. New York: Gallimard, 1989.

Don't lose these pocket editions—a theme developed in a book that fits in your pocket! This is one of a series that introduces readers to varieties of animals and plants found at the shore and describes their habitat among rocks, tides, and sand. Almost any other theme imaginable can be found in this series.

Lenga, Rosalind. *The Amazing Fact Book of Fish.* Illustrated by Norman Weaver. Mankato, Minn.: Creative Education, 1988.

Various species of ocean fish are examined through magnificently detailed illustrations and factual text.

Limmer, Mary Jane. *Where Will You Swim Tonight?* Illustrated by Helena Clare Pittman. Niles, Ill.: Whitman, 1991.

This bedtime story fantasy invites children to swim with six prickly blowfish, seven slippery eels, and nine lumpy oysters. A brief but entertaining introduction to the life of the sea.

Maestro, Betsy. *A Sea Full of Sharks.* Illustrated by Giulio Maestro. New York: Scholastic, 1990.

Out of all the sea creatures, children are most fascinated by sharks. Ranging in size from six inches to sixty feet, sharks and their world are introduced to young children in this book.

Mainig, Anita. *Where the Waves Break: Life at the Edge of the Sea.* Minneapolis, Minn.: Carolrhoda, 1985.

Through color close-ups of life along the edge of the sea, readers discover a whole new world within their reach.

Seymour, Peter. *What's in the Deep Blue Sea?* Illustrated by David A. Carter. New York: Holt, 1990.

A jiggly jellyfish, two squiggly squids, and even a shy seahorse lurk behind the masterful design of this ingenious pop-up book. Vibrant, colorful illustrations mesmerize even the adult in this hide-and-seek book.

What's Inside? Shells. New York: Dorling Kindersley, 1991.

An especially good series that is designed to help young children understand what's underneath a shell. It shows how an oyster makes a pearl, what a tortoise looks like under his shell, and the inner workings of a crab's claw. Others in this series include: *What's Inside My Body?, What's Inside Small Animals?, What's Inside Toys?*

Wood, John Norris. *Nature Hide & Seeks: OCEANS.* New York: Knopf, 1985.

Lurking in weeds, concealed in darkness, and buried in sand, fascinating creatures of the sea are camouflaged in coral reefs. Through the fold-out flaps, you can dive in and discover nature's strangest and most wonderful creatures. A unique format that would add to any ocean display.

The Seasons

Allison, Linda. *The Sierra Club Summer Book/The Reasons for Seasons.* Boston: Little, Brown, 1989, 1975.

A fun-filled nature and craft book, *The Sierra Club Summer Book* features such exciting and entertaining activities as building bird feeders, constructing water slides, cooking eggs on the sidewalk, and bottle art.

From invisible ink to window salad, *The Reasons for Seasons* contains a veritable potpourri of science experiments, all of which contribute to an understanding of the seasons and their effect on the earth.

Ball, Jacqueline A. *What Can It Be? Riddles About the Seasons.* Eden Prairie, Minn.: Silver, 1989.

"Munch me at snack time, crunch me at lunch . . . what am I?" Rhyming poem-riddles spark an interest in the four seasons.

Bjork, Christina. *Linnea's Almanac.* Illustrated by Lena Anderson. New York: R&S Books, 1989.

A monthly scrapbook of Linnea's indoor and outdoor activities for a year. She opens a bird restaurant in January, finds the first spring flower in March, goes beach combing in July, and makes her own Christmas presents in December. Filled with entertaining and exciting ideas—even adults will learn something new.

Coxe, Jolly. *Whose Footprints?* New York: Crowell, 1990.

A enjoyable journey for the youngest reader, as a mother and daughter take a walk through the snow and discover different footprints animals have left behind.

Leslie, Clare W. *Nature All Year Long.* New York: Greenwillow, 1991.

The 12 months of nature in all her splendor are illustrated in this spectacular book which focuses on imaginative ideas and monthly activities that will enthrall all readers.

Maass, Robert. *When Autumn Comes.* New York: Holt, 1990.

Photographs and simple words depict the coming of fall and the change of the seasons. Provides a beautiful glimpse of New England in America.

Rockwell, Anne. *First Comes Spring.* New York: Crowell, 1985.

A celebration of the seasons for the youngest reader. Simple text and bright, colorful pictures illustrate how a bear's world changes throughout the year.

Schwartz, David. *Hidden Life of the Pond.* Photographs by Dwight Kuhn. New York: Crown/Random House, 1988.

Beginning with the spring rains and ending with the coming of winter, this special book presents a wide array of life on the pond.

Webster, Harriet. *Winter Book.* Illustrated by Irene Trivas. New York: Aladdin, 1988.

Learn to track wild animals, study snowflakes, and make Indian pudding in this collection of activities, observations, and information celebrating the winter season. Includes a discussion of the season's holidays.

York, Jane, ed. *Seasons.* The My First Look At Series. New York: Random House, 1990.

A well designed book with bright, clear photographs of objects, plants, and animals depicting the seasons and their highlights. For the enjoyment of the youngest reader.

Other books in the series include *Colors, Opposites, Touch, Home, Shapes, Numbers,* and *Sizes.*

Trees

Behn, Harry. *Trees.* Illustrated by James Endicott. New York: Holt, 1992.

Printed on recycled paper, this eloquent poem encourages young children to look with wonder and respect at the grandeur of trees. Stunning illustrations beautifully complement this rhythmic poem.

Ehlert, Lois. *Red Leaf, Yellow Leaf.* New York: Harcourt Brace Jovanovich: 1991.

A child's relationship with a sugar maple tree is beautifully described and illustrated in Ehlert's distinctive and unique style. Also highlights and describes specific parts of a tree, including the bark and sap, and includes information about planting your own tree.

Florian, Douglas. *Discovering Trees.* New York: Aladdin, 1986.

Colorful drawings and factual text create a good introduction to trees, their growth, reproduction, and importance. Specific trees highlighted include the baobab, the bald cypress, the ginkgo, and the date palm tree.

Fowler, Allan. *It Could Still Be a Tree.* Chicago: Children's Press, 1990.

A perfect guide for identifying trees for the very young child. Examples of evergreens, maples, and redwoods. A great small size.

Hindley, Judy. *The Tree.* Illustrated by Alison Wisenfield. New York: Potter, 1990.

Engaging design and illustrations, along with lyrical text, provide interesting information about different types of trees, including the hawthorn, the sycamore, and the beech. A rhyming poem about each tree accompanies each description. A beautiful book portraying the beauty of trees.

Hiscock, Bruce. *The Big Tree.* New York: Atheneum, 1991.

A history lesson that focuses on the growth of an old maple tree from a seed during the American Revolution to its maturity in contemporary times.

Jeunesse, Gallimard, and de Bourgoing, Pascale. *The Tree.* Illustrated by P.M. Valet. Cartwheel Book Series. New York: Scholastic, 1992.

Originally published in France, these uniquely spiral-bound books with plastic overlays are truly "magic." You can "look directly into an apple, a tree, an egg, a flower . . . all with the turn of a brightly painted transparent page."
Other books in the series include *Colors, Fruit, The Ladybug and Other Insects, Weather,* and *The Egg.*

Lasky, Kathryn. *Sugaring Time.* Photographs by Christopher G. Knight. New York: Macmillan, 1986.

A fine collaboration between photographer and writer. Readable text illustrates how sap is tapped from maple trees and processed into maple syrup.

Maestro, Betsy. *How Do Apples Grow?* Illustrated by Giulio Maestro. New York: Harper Collins, 1992.

A revised edition of an old favorite! A charming introduction to an essential life cycle of the apple.

Micucci, Charles. *Apples*. New York: Orchard, 1992.

Presents in a unique picture format a variety of facts about apples, including how they grow, crossbreeding and grafting techniques, harvesting practices, and a potpourri of other interesting facts about apples. Includes an entertaining version of the legend of Johnny Appleseed.

Parnall, Peter. *Apple Tree*. New York: Macmillan, 1988.

A seasonal depiction of an apple tree's encounters with the elements, animals, and man during a year of its life. Beautiful full-page drawings and poetic text.

Watts, Barrie. *Apple Tree*. Morristown, N.J.: Silver Burdette, 1986.

Describes in close-up photographs and simple text how an apple develops from blossoms in the spring to ripe fruits in the fall.

Water

Ardley, Neil. *The Science Book of Water*. New York: Harcourt Brace Jovanovich, 1991.

Demonstrates the properties of water through clear, color photographs. Each experiment can be easily followed step by step by a young child. Catch an ice cube with a string, watch oil rise, or make a water volcano.

―――. *The Science Book of Weather*. New York: Harcourt Brace Jovanovich, 1992.

How to make rain and rainbows, or how to form mist or make frost is clearly described in easy-to-follow photographs. Appropriate format for young children.

Basic Starters Series. *Rain.* London: Macdonald & Co., 1971.

A wonderful resource for children of all the possible effects rain may have in their lives. Very brief text, excellent illustrations. Every page can be a source for discussion.

Bounici, Peter. *The First Rains.* Illustrated by Lisa Kopper. Minneapolis, Minn.: Carolrhoda Books, Inc., 1985.

A simple story of waiting for the rains to come to India. Powerfully illustrates the importance of water in peoples' lives.

Brandt, Keith. *What Makes It Rain? The Story of a Raindrop.* Illustrated by Yoshi Miyake. Mahwah, N.J.: Troll Associates, 1982.

A story of how water appears in nature (e.g., rain drops, rivers, puddles, clouds) with lovely illustrations.

Brauleis, Franklyn M. *Floating and Sinking.* Illustrated by Robert Galster. New York: Thomas Crowell, 1967.

Cole, Joanna. *The Magic School Bus at the Waterworks.* Illustrated by Bruce Degen. New York: Scholastic, Inc., 1986.

"The Magic School Bus" series combines "facts" with children's "fantasies." This time the bus takes them around the city to find out where and how running water originates before it comes to our faucet. Although it is written for children in the primary grades, it can be part of a classroom of 4–5 year olds. The illustrations are explicit and engage children's curiosity.

Howell, Ruth. *Splash and Flow.* Photos by Arline Strong. New York: Atheneum, 1973.

Photos and text describe many ways water affects people's lives, such as rain, running under a sprinkler, ice, cooking, washing, putting out fires.

Jane, Simon. *Dear Mr. Blueberry*. New York: McElderry Books, 1991.

In letter-writing format, Emily learns that a whale cannot possibly live in her pond and that whales need salt water. Imaginative, child-like text! (Also could be used with ocean unit on whales.)

Leutscher, Alfred. *Water*. Pictures by Nick Hardcastle. New York: The Dial Press, 1983.

The author invites readers to take a close look at water in its many forms. The text might be lengthy for young children, but the illustrations convey the concepts, and the teacher may use it as a source for discussion.

Pine, Tillie S., and Joseph Levine. *Water All Around Us*. Illustrated by Bernice Myers. New York: Whittlesey House, 1959.

Teaches about the properties of water with stories, pictures, and simple ideas for activities.

Rain and Hail. Illustrated by Harriett Barton. New York: Thomas Crowell, 1983.

A very simple explanation of how rain and other forms of precipitation are formed. Clear, colorful illustrations.

Snow Is Falling. Illustrated by Holly Keller. New York: Harper & Row, 1986.

A "find-out-about-snow" story. How it changes nature (people, animals, plants) and what happens when it gets warmer. The text and the illustrations present concrete experiences to children which could easily be part of their own lives.

Taylor, Barbara. *Pond Life*. Look Closer Series. New York: Dorling Kindersley, 1992.

Through clear, close-up photographs, life in a pond takes on new dimensions. Format is especially luring for young children.

Weather and the Elements

Ardley, Neil. *The Science Book of Air/The Science Book of Water*. New York: Harcourt Brace Jovanovich, 1991.

In *The Science Book of Air*, several interesting and illuminating experiments demonstrate the principles of air and flight. Full color, clear photographs give step-by-step instructions for each experiment.

The Science Book of Water demonstrates the properties of water through clear, color photographs. Each experiment can be easily followed step by step by a young child. Catch an ice cube with a string, watch foil rise, or make a water volcano.

Branley, Franklyn. *It's Raining Cats and Dogs*. Illustrated by True Kelley. Boston: Houghton Mifflin, 1987.

A potpourri of interesting and amazing weather phenomena, facts and folklore, and dramatic weather events. Read about hurricanes, tornadoes, and why lightning never strikes twice.

Dorros, Arthur. *Feel the Wind*. New York: Harper & Row, 1989.

From gentle breezes to powerful hurricanes, find out all about the wind—what causes it, how it can be used to help us, and how it affects our weather. Even learn to make your own weather vane.

Gibbons, Gail. *Catch the Wind: All About Kites*. Boston: Little, Brown, 1989.

An introduction to wind and kites, especially how to make your own kite, and even how to launch it! Written in the typical, clear Gibbons format.

Gibbons, Gail. *Weather Words and What They Mean*. New York: Holiday House, 1990.

A brightly illustrated dictionary of common weather terms, including air pressure, moisture, and blizzard. A list of curious weather facts concludes the book.

McVey, Vicky. *The Sierra Club Book of Weatherwisdom*. Illustrated by Martha Weston. Boston: Little, Brown, 1991.

A lively discussion of climates and seasons, wind and rain, warm and cold fronts, atmospheric pressure, and weather prediction. Features activities, games, and experiments.

Peters, Lisa Westburg. *Water's Way*. Illustrated by Ted Rand. New York: Arcade.

Discusses different forms that water can have—from clouds to steam to fog. For the youngest reader.
Other titles in the series include *Light* and *Color*.

V

Science Education
for the Special Child

This essay examines current thinking on science education for the special child and the key resources that are available in that area. During the last 25 years in particular there have been challenges to involve special children in effective learning. There have also been struggles and victories concerning the best way to accomplish this goal. Legislation has been passed that entitles *all* children to equal opportunity in education.

Literature supports the notion that learning science is essential for children's growth and development, and especially for young children's sensory approaches in exploring the world around them. During the action-based interactive process that is science learning, children develop process skills in observing, relating, sorting, classifying, comparing, and predicting—all so necessary in understanding and appreciating physical objects, natural phenomena, and living things.

These assumptions, about how young children's involvement with science contributes to their development, gain a new dimension when we think of special children. This is particularly so because the term includes children with a wide range of handicaps—physical, emotional, and intellectual. These needs therefore mandate a stronger emphasis in the planning of the children's educational experiences so that they may be provided with compensatory and therapeutic activities that will enable them to live fuller lives in a world so compact with knowledge and problem solving possibilities.

Many science educators have addressed the issue of teaching science to special children; more specifically, the National Science Teachers' Association (NSTA) devoted an entire conference to the exploration and documentation of the role of science in the lives of physically handicapped children. During this 1978 NSTA conference in Washington, D.C., a wide range of information was presented that included evidence of the importance of teaching science to children with visual, auditory, and orthopedic impairments. In conclusion the conferees agreed on the need for more science teaching in the learning environments of special children and recommended to teachers a wide range of sources on how and where to seek assistance in enriching their teaching of science. A bibliography and an exhaustive list of organizations that concern themselves with science and the handicapped are also included in their publication *Sourcebook Science Education and the Physically Handicapped*. The book is a valuable companion to all professionals who focus their teaching on special children.

The compensatory approach in teaching science to special children is the theme of Haldary and Cohen in their monumental book *Laboratory Science and Art for Blind, Deaf and Emotionally Disturbed Children*. The book is written for preservice and inservice teachers who plan to meet the needs of the handicapped child in or out of the classroom. The science activities that compensate for certain handicaps are adapted from well-known elementary science curricula: ESS (Elementary Science Study), S-APA (Science-A Process Approach), and SCIS (Science Curriculum Improvement Study). The authors underscore the importance of understanding the handicap, the physical and emotional limitations of the child, and what adaptations are required to meet the child's needs so that s/he can enjoy effective learning.

Furthermore, a strong argument is presented in Haldary and Cohen for the ways in which art and science "share common learning experiences and procedures" and how discoveries in science can be reinforced through art projects.

This interplay between the two disciplines facilitates further children's understanding of the nature of the physical world and its natural phenomena. For example, in testing the floating and sinking concept by making clay boats in a water table, a blind child can explore different shapes and how they relate to sinking and floating. These tactile observations can be clarified through an art project in wooden boat building and wood carving, in which the child creates the simple, representational form of a boat. Thus, the interrelatedness of science and art can help the handicapped child expand upon his tactile experience and further clarify the physical properties of floating and sinking structures. This relationship between science and art can be exploited to equal advantage with emotionally disturbed children. What it provides is both a structure for the understanding of physical properties and natural phenomena and an outlet for artistic expression. Furthermore, the sense of control they experience will enhance their confidence and self-esteem and will contribute therapeutically to their development.

The emphasis on the adaptation of science activities to accommodate the needs of special children finds strong support in Mary Rowe's writing. She highlights the concept of time as an important variable in the teaching of science for special children. The mentally retarded need more time to explore and integrate their findings, the emotionally disturbed need more time to control their responses, deaf children are slower in picking out visual information through lip reading, and blind students have "no lead time." According to Rowe, teaching science to the handicapped is more important than it is for children without handicaps. She claims that the physical world is not as available to them as to other children. Experiences that lead to exploration, observation, classification, and measurement must be created so that children with handicaps will have an equal opportunity to learn about the world around them.

The following books clearly show the important role science plays in the development of a child with special needs. Although there are different opinions in the field, the works discussed in this essay and those listed in the bibliography provide a foundation that can be used as a springboard to more complete knowledge of the role of science in the education of special children.

BIBLIOGRAPHY

Brearley, M., et al. *The Teaching of Young Children.* New York: Schocken, 1969.

Flavell, John H. *Developmental Psychology of Jean Piaget.* New York: Van Nostrand, 1963.

Haldary, D.F., and S.H. Cohen. *Laboratory Science and Art for Blind, Deaf and Emotionally Disturbed Children.* Baltimore, Md.: Baltimore UP, 1978.

Hawkins, D. "Messing About in Science." *Science and Children* 2 (February 1969): 5–9.

Hein, G. "Children's Science Is Another Culture." *Technology Review.* 1968.

Hochman, V., and M. Greenwald. *Science Experiences in Early Childhood.* New York: Bank Street College of Education Publications, 1963.

Hoffman, H.H., and K.S. Ricker. *Sourcebook in Science Education and the Physically Handicapped.* Washington, D.C.: NSTA, 1979.

Landsdown, B., P.E. Blackwood, and P.F. Brandwein. *Teaching Elementary Science Through Investigation and Colloquium.* New York: Harcourt Brace Jovanovich, 1971.

McIntyre, M. *Early Childhood and Science.* Washington, D.C.: NSTA, 1984.

Piaget, J. *The Child and Reality.* New York: Grossman Publishers, 1972.

Rowe, Mary Budd. "Help Is Desired to Those in Need." *Science and Children* 12 (March 1975): 23–25.

Rowe, Mary Budd. *Teaching Science as Continuous Inquiry: A Basic.* New York: McGraw-Hill, 1978.

Index

SOURCE BOOKS ON EDUCATION